I WONDER IF CHOCOLATE KILLS BRAIN CELLS

I Wonder
If Chocolate Kills
Brain Cells

ANDREW WOODING

KINGSWAY PUBLICATIONS

EASTBOURNE

ISBN 0 86065 562 8

Biblical quotations are from
the Holy Bible: New International Version,
copyright © International Bible Society 1973, 1978, 1984

Printed in Great Britain for
KINGSWAY PUBLICATIONS LTD
Lottbridge Drove, Eastbourne, E. Sussex BN23 6NT by
Cox & Wyman Ltd, Reading.
Typeset by Nuprint Ltd, Harpenden, Herts AL5 4SE.

To my grandparents:
Nanny Knight and Nanna and Grandad Wooding

And to small group one:
Annette Dunham, Laurie Falco, Helen Kaufmann,
Rachel Meakin, Dominique Monbaron,
Keith Patrick and Terri Plater

Contents

Foreword by Loren Cunningham   9

Acknowledgements   10

Author's Note   12

The Discipleship Training School   13

Copenhagen   87

The GO Festival   125

The Sentimental Conclusion   155

Foreword

Everyone appreciates the person who can poke fun at himself. Andrew has written with gentle humour his account of being in YWAM. He has shown us that God does indeed use us—even when we are young and make mistakes. Still, somehow, his work gets done and we, like Andrew, are changed in the process.

This light-hearted account of short-term missions gives the story through the average young person's eyes—not the heroic, pith-helmeted missionary's. Just a young person who swallows his fears and shortcomings and says, 'Here I am, Lord, send me.'

Loren Cunningham
President, Youth With A Mission

Acknowledgements

Thanks to everyone who helped me in California while I was writing this book: Geoff Booker, Muriel Burgert, Dianna Burhans, Bruce and Anna Butler, Eddie Cairns, Mary Chapeau, Cinder, Gavin Connolly, Tom and Pita Delamater, Jeff and Palma Fitch, Lane Harris, Jan Jensen, Jason Martin, Susan Martin, Kathy McCoy, Muffin, everyone at the Open Doors office in Santa Ana, Linda Peterson, Tim and Pat Phillips, Elizabeth Poklacki, Ray and Brenda Poklacki, Dennis Richmond, Lois Sanborn, Ed and Marybelle Steele, Patty Wilkinson, Dan and Norma Wooding (my parents) and Peter Wooding (my brother).

Thanks to my friend, Christopher Catherwood, without whose regular letters of encouragement this book would never have been written; to Jim and Janice Rogers for their wise editorial suggestions; and a special thank you to Loren Cunningham, who has been an example for so many young (and not so young) people, including me!

I'd also like to thank all the wonderful people I met

while in YWAM; every single one of my relatives and friends; all the people over the years that I've learnt from and admire; everyone who's ever been involved in the manufacture of chocolate or chocolate-related products; and the entire human race. I think that covers it.

God bless you all!

Author's Note

Okay. Confession time. I didn't actually keep a diary for most of my time with Youth With A Mission, so the bulk of this book was written from memory. And my memory is about as reliable as a British Rail timetable, so this book is far from inerrant.

About 95% of the book is true. In many places I've knowingly shuffled events from one date to another for the sake of pacing. And I can't remember every word of every conversation, or what we had for dinner on a certain day, so I've taken the liberty of filling in a few gaps with made-up occurrences.

Rest assured, the more unusual the event the more likely it is to be true!

The
Discipleship Training
School

14th May (Monday):

I don't remember much of the journey to Holmsted Manor this afternoon. An old schoolfriend from Walton-on-Thames volunteered to drive me there, and I must have spent most of the time nodding my head at his stories while practising not looking petrified. We eventually said 'goodbye' when he dropped me off at Holmsted, and then my suitcases and I were escorted up to what is to be my dormitory for the next ten weeks (room 60—one of two boys' dormitories). I have to share it with six other men. Yuck!

In the evening (after exploring the grounds for the previous few hours and generally trying to hide from everyone), all of us met in the dining area and were briefly welcomed to this Discipleship Training School (or DTS) by one of the school leaders. Then, after singing some praise songs, we had to introduce ourselves one-by-one. Everyone here seems so much older and more clever than me. I hope none of them find out that I'm not really a very good Christian.

I briefly visited the snack bar a few moments ago and experienced both paranoia and claustrophobia at the same time. So here I am now under the stars, sitting alone on the cool grass outside while nervously crunching my Polos.

I dread going up to that dormitory before 'lights out' at 11 o'clock. What on earth have I let myself in for?

15th May (Tuesday):

What an abysmal night I had last night. I couldn't get to sleep at all. Breakfast was rotten. What I thought was semolina turned out to be very strong home-made yoghurt. It definitely didn't go well with the corn-flakes. And I didn't really feel much like praying during 'quiet time' so I wrote a letter to my parents in California.

Our first lecture was 'Spiritual Growth'—which was intimidating to say the least! Basically the lecturer told us that God has taken us out of our comfortable everyday existences for the next three-and-a-half months, and is going to allow all our faults and weaknesses to rise to the surface so that he can deal with them. *My* main weakness is chocolate. I hope it doesn't rise to the surface too often!

After lunch we had our first two-and-a-half-hour afternoon work period which consisted of all the male students tramping round the freezing-cold grounds of Holmsted while a leader told us all the jobs that need to be done. On our way back to the house I prayed my first real prayer since the start of the DTS: 'Lord, don't make me work on the grounds!' I mentally devised an escape plan from Holmsted during our free time after dinner.

We met in the dining area again this evening for another one of those introductory meetings. And then there was another mad rush for the snack bar.

I wish the weather would perk up a bit. It's almost too cold to write out here.

16th May (Wednesday):

My first YWAM miracle! I've been assigned to the tape department for the rest of the DTS and I don't have to work on the grounds at all! Praise the Lord, and all that kind of stuff! Wooh!

We didn't have a lecture this morning. Instead we were treated to a short account of the history of YWAM and then shown video tapes from different YWAM bases around the world. I'm impressed, and I didn't realize that YWAM was such a big operation. Afterwards we were asked what we'd most like to accomplish during the DTS. I said 'to finish it', and everyone laughed.

I'm proud of myself. After another one of those evening meetings, I braved a whole game of Ludo in the snack bar. I'm also writing this diary entry in the warmth of our dormitory for the first time. I hope the sound of me crunching Polos doesn't wake everyone up.

17th May (Thursday):

Our lecture this morning was on 'Note Taking', and it was probably very good. I can't tell you much about it, though, since I fell asleep after five minutes and didn't take any notes.

After the lecture I called my parents in California and found out that Dad'll be visiting England in a few weeks—which is great news! Dad also promised to bring me some up-to-date information on the new *Star Trek* film. I hope Mr Spock comes back to life.

Working in that tape department is a cinch. All I have to do is type cassette labels and duplicate tapes. There *is* a slight disadvantage, though. My supervisor walked in this morning and said: 'Pooh! What an awful smell!' At first I thought he meant me, but then he explained: 'It's probably a dead rat behind the wall. There was one there last year, and it took us ages to find it.'

I premiered my Winston Churchill impression at the dinner table today, but it wasn't greeted with quite the rapturous acclaim that I'd hoped for. Most people thought I was coughing.

18th May (Friday):

I decided to have my quiet time outside in the cold this morning so that I wouldn't fall asleep...and guess what? I started by reading Proverbs 1 on the grass, lay down so that I'd be more comfortable while praying, and then....Well, luckily I woke up in time for this morning's first lecture on how to have a quiet time. Needless to say, one of the things we were advised *not* to do during a quiet time was fall asleep. I was tempted to ask one of the leaders to pray with me about this, but I was too tired.

After the evening meal (scrumptious lasagne!), I decided to explore the West Sussex countryside outside Holmsted for the first time, and saw rather more of it than I'd intended. I got lost along a muddy public footpath, and pessimistically concluded after two hours of going round in circles and the sun rapidly setting that I would never see civilization again. Finally, though, I managed to reach a road, and there was just enough light in the sky for me to stagger back to Holmsted in time for the opening of the snack bar. I promptly took my frustrations out on a Mars bar. I hope it didn't mind.

19th May (Saturday):

All of us were driven to Crawley this morning, which was a definite breath of fresh air (metaphorically speaking, of course). I've lived most of my life in cities, and after being stranded in remote countryside for a whole five days, it was good to see real concrete and junk food places again. After a pleasant walk through town, luxuriously inhaling the glorious carbon monoxide, I quickly stocked up on comics and a Spike Milligan book before being reluctantly whisked back to boring old nature and clean air.

In the evening the whole DTS was driven up to London to attend a special celebration service at a church there—which was quite fun. When we returned to Holmsted, however, we found our toothpaste tubes sabotaged and all the lightbulbs missing from our dormitories.

The previous DTS returned from their outreach in Paris today, and are sleeping outside in the barn. Some students suspect that these strange occurrences and the return of this DTS might possibly be related. I think they may be right.

20th May (Sunday):

Nothing much happened today. After church I read one of the comics that I bought in Crawley, and then I went for a walk. That's about it. Sorry my day was so boring.

The previous DTS got a taste of their own medicine this morning. Two of *our* students secretly turned off their gas supply, and also stole their breakfasts. Luckily they didn't retaliate, and I'm glad they took it well. If someone stole *my* breakfast I would have... I would have gone away somewhere and sulked.

21st May (Monday):

We students have now been split up into permanent discussion or 'small groups' that will meet every weekday until the end of the DTS. I'm in small group one which is led by Keith and Laurie, and I was rather intimidated at first since the other seven in the group are older than me. Soon, though, I discovered that they're actually quite friendly—and they even liked my 'Tarzan' joke!

I had my hair cut today. Laurie was kind enough to cut it for free, but she insisted that I have a parting. I didn't have the heart to tell her that I thought it looked cissy, so I let her cut it *her* way then combed it out afterwards. I'm going to have to avoid her over the next few days.

We've started praying in our dormitory every night at 10.30 which means less time in the snack bar beating people at Ludo. Frankly, I'm annoyed.

22nd May (Tuesday):

I had a wonderful dream last night; the most beautiful dream I've ever had. I saw a man dressed in Arabian-type clothes, sitting on a radiator in a Holmsted Manor corridor while hugging lots of happy children that were laughing and dancing around him. I walked closer to him in my dream, and when he looked up and smiled at me I knew immediately who he was. There was so much love in that smile that it almost broke my heart. He beckoned me closer, took me in his arms, and Jesus hugged me there and then with as much love and acceptance as he'd hugged all his other children. God actually loves me. Wow.

Despite this, I'm depressed. It was the turn of small groups one and two to go on outreach this evening, and we had to walk round Brighton in pairs to invite people back to our coffee bar. My partner was Laurie, and she did great—but *I* was an absolute dimbo. While I timidly observed all, she preached to a Muslim guy on the street, brought him back to the coffee bar, preached to him a bit more, prayed with him, then handed him an Arabic New Testament which he promised to read and think about. I kept wanting to help her, but just couldn't think of anything to say. My only contribution to the evening was making three cups of coffee for us, and even they weren't all that good.

23rd May (Wednesday):

I felt absolutely dreadful this morning (mainly because I didn't get much sleep after the outreach last night), and I couldn't communicate properly at the breakfast table. Then I had my first shave since the start of the DTS and cut myself in five places. I misjudged where my nose was, and blood was dripping everywhere. I also forgot that today was memory verse day. Before each Wednesday morning lecture, individual students are chosen to recite the Bible verse that was given them the previous week to learn. Much to my embarrassment I was the first student to be chosen today, and I was also apparently the only student who'd forgotten to memorize 1 John 1:9.

Small group time was rotten. Laurie noticed that I'd combed away that parting she'd so skilfully cut for me—and she wasn't too pleased. Keith wasn't pleased with me either. He's the person in charge of memory verses. Soon we all started talking about last night's outreach, and apparently everyone else really enjoyed themselves and had great conversations with people on the streets—which made me feel bad. Then I had to work in that tape department which now smells even worse.

In the evening we had our first weekly drama period. Although we didn't rehearse any dramas (just watched a video of the dramas the prevoius DTS had put together), I was petrified of what we were told we're going to be doing. Singing and drama on the streets! Yuck. Afterwards I met privately with Keith and Laurie. (They have to meet once a week with each member of their small group.) They asked me if I was having any problems so far on the DTS, and I lied by saying 'no' because I didn't feel much like talking.

I don't know how all those characters in the Bible coped during *their* difficult times, but *I'm* doing terribly.

24th May (Thursday):

Small group time was a little better today. We nattered a lot about train spotting and pop music, which meant there was less time devoted to depressing spiritual matters that make me feel inferior. I also discovered that one of the members of our small group is the person in charge of the snack bar. She has the authority to give away free goodies, so I've decided to get to know her a little better.

I went up for prayer after this evening's lecture on 'The Father Heart of God', and to my surprise a great feeling of peace flowed right through me. Afterwards, the person who'd prayed for me said: 'Andrew, the Lord has done more work in your life these last few days than many Christians have received in their lifetime. And there's going to be more, so be open to receive it.'

Unfortunately it looks like I've had more chocolate than most Christians as well. I'm sadly putting on weight.

25th May (Friday):

I'm beginning to like this DTS. I enjoyed talking to people at the breakfast table for once, I stayed awake for the whole of my quiet time (a minor miracle!), and I thoroughly enjoyed this morning's lecture on 'The Character of God'. I hadn't realized before just how much God loves us and wants to help us individually in our everyday lives.

Two small groups (but luckily not ours) did some outreach in Brighton tonight, and an intercession group was arranged for those who stayed behind and wanted to pray for them. I ran into the prayer room a bit late, tripped over a chair, did a double somersault, said a few naughty words that I had to apologize for afterwards, and landed in an embarrassed heap by the window. (Everyone except me found this highly amusing.) This was soon forgotten, thank goodness, and during our prayer time I experienced a closeness to God that I haven't felt much before. This prayer business is actually quite fun.

I played Scrabble with that person in charge of the snack bar afterwards, and I'm ashamed to say that she absolutely thrashed me. It seems like she knows the whole of the Oxford dictionary off by heart! I'm going to have to play against her again. She's definitely not going to get away with this.

26th May (Saturday):

There was a horrible smell in the dormitory this morning. I thought it might be all those unwashed clothes in my cupboard, so I went down to the laundry room to wash them and spent most of the morning there. Consequently I missed the coach trip to Crawley, which was a shame because I missed out on this week's comics. This loss was made up for, though, by a showing of *The Return of the Man From U.N.C.L.E.* in the dining room this evening. I can't honestly say that it was the best film I've seen (in fact, it was one of the worst!), but it was fun in a stupid sort of way.

I suggested to the social director what our next video should be, but he's obviously not a *Star Trek* fan.

27th May (Sunday):

Woke up, went to church, walked round the grounds for a while, listened to Billy Graham on the radio, played Ludo in the snack bar, prayed in our dormitory, then went to sleep.

This has got to be one of the most boring diary entries so far, but it's also been one of my most enjoyable days. Isn't that interesting.

28th May (Monday):

Every Monday morning everyone in Holmsted Manor—students, group leaders and house staff—meets in the dining area for an hour-long session of praise and worship to start off the week. I wish they'd have it in the evening instead. I can't take looking at so many smiling faces so early in the morning.

After this morning's session, we had our first lecture on 'Prayer'. Most of this week's lectures are going to be about prayer of one sort or another, and since regular times of intercession are going to be starting next week I'm now going to have to take proper notes instead of day-dreaming or falling asleep at the back of the room.

I called Mum in America this evening, and she asked me lots of really important questions like whether I've had my hair cut yet and if I'm eating enough. 'Yes,' I said to her first question. Then I miserably looked down at my stomach and had to answer the second question in the affirmative too. To comfort me in my affliction, I bought myself a Mars bar.

29th May (Tuesday):

Last week we were each handed a leaflet on different types of sins, and were told to write down on the back of it all the sins we feel we're guilty of. This morning they were all collected, and we gathered outside to burn them in a wheelbarrow while praying and singing praise songs. It was a symbolic act, our leader explained, to show God that we're turning our backs on our sinful nature. A good idea, I thought, except that I'd forgotten to fill in *my* leaflet and didn't have time to rectify this before handing it in. All that was burnt was a doodle I'd made of a snail smoking a pipe. Another great loss to the art world, I'm afraid.

I won a game of Scrabble in the snack bar this evening, but it wasn't against that girl in our small group. I'm going to challenge her to another game soon, so keep reading for details of my upcoming victory.

30th May (Wednesday):

I forgot to learn the memory verse again today (Luke 10:27), and Keith deliberately picked me to recite it because he remembered the mess I'd made of it last week. After two humiliations now, I finally have a repentant heart. While in the tape department, I read 1 John 5:14–15 over and over again (next week's memory verses) until they'd finally sunk in. Then I went over to Keith during dinner to recite what I'd learnt. Unfortunately I forgot every single word, and returned to my own dinner table in shame. Keith looked quite amused, though.

More drama this evening, unfortunately—although

we still didn't have to rehearse anything. We just chose which of the short dances or dramas we wanted to be in, then went away in groups to read our scripts and commit our performances to the Lord. We had aerobics afterwards, and I got the giggles because I kept getting everything wrong. (I wasn't the only one!) I was also out of breath, and still am. I'm definitely going to have to lose weight.

31st May (Thursday):

I discovered the children's play area during quiet time this morning, and had great fun trying to get as high as I could on the swings and getting stuck on the slide. I didn't really do much praying or Bible reading, but at least I didn't fall asleep.

We played volley-ball during small group time, and it wasn't as hard as I thought it would be. There's going to be a volley-ball tournament soon between all the small groups, and I'm pretty confident that we're going to win—I can feel it in my spirit. This is my first incident of guidance during the DTS. I hope I'm right. I haven't been doing too well in hearing from the Lord during my quiet times, so this would be a tremendous boost to my confidence.

1st June (Friday):

My entire notes for the two lectures this morning were doodles of a man pulling a face and an overweight elephant riding a bicycle. I felt a bit guilty about this until a Norwegian showed me *his* notes: an aeroplane fight in the skies during World War I, and Sylvester Stallone. I'll probably be a master artist by the end of this DTS.

Small group time was fun. We talked about the picnic we'll be having together tomorrow which I'm really looking forward to. Work duty was quite relaxing as well, especially since it was pouring with rain outside and I had the smug satisfaction of being *inside* in the small heated tape department. The only disadvantage was that awful smell which is getting worse by the minute.

Sorry my handwriting's a bit shaky. I'm writing this in the van on the way to our small group's outreach in Leicester Square. We get back very late tonight, so I'll tell you how we get along in tomorrow's entry. If diaries could pray, I'd ask you to pray for me. I'm very nervous about the whole thing.

2nd June (Saturday):

I don't really want to write about last night. Ugh. What a failure I was. Three whole hours in freezing Leicester Square, with people hurling abuse at us all the time and me shivering at the back pretending I wasn't in YWAM at all and was just a normal agnostic like everyone else. We even got stopped by the police, and for one awful moment I thought we were going to spend the night in jail. I tried to witness to people, but my mouth just sort of froze up, and once again my partner had to do all the work.

Let me talk about our small group's picnic instead. That was much more pleasant.

First we drove to Arundel Castle, but discovered that it was closed (much to my relief—castles send me to sleep). Instead we went for a walk around town, and then had our picnic by a river. After we'd devoured all our goodies (including the tin of custard I'd bought in

28

town) we lay down in the sun recovering. The New Zealander in our group told us that when it's hot, custard turns into insects in your stomach. For some reason, I found it hard to relax after that.

Then on to Littlehampton where a few of us went swimming (but not me), and the rest of us had an exciting watermelon pip spitting contest. I accidentally got Keith on the nose, which he wasn't too pleased about. Then we returned to Holmsted, and met up in room 63 (one of the leaders' rooms) for a goodnight cup of coffee and some chocolate digestives.

In spite of myself, I'm actually beginning to like this small group. Being with them is just like having fun at school again. My innocence and sense of humour is returning—and I like it.

3rd June (Sunday):

Depression set in this morning. This always happens after I've had a good day. I played another game of Scrabble with that girl from the snack bar in the afternoon, which cheered me up a bit even though she thrashed me just like before. But most of the rest of the day I felt alone, inadequate, inferior, and other sorts of fun stuff like that.

In the evening I went for a prayerful walk around the grounds of Holmsted. I desperately wanted some encouragement from God, so I left my Bible open on a bench by the driveway and asked the Lord to make the wind blow the pages to a section he wanted me to read. In the meantime I walked up and down the driveway praying out loud and confessing various sins. After nearly an hour of this I returned to the bench—and just as I sat down a sudden gust of wind blew my Bible open to the first verse of John 14: 'Do not let your hearts be troubled. Trust in God; trust also in me.' The words seemed to leap out of the page as I read them, and I knew that the Lord wanted me to be comforted by them. Hallelujah! I'm not depressed any more.

Why is it that my emotions are always up and down?

4th June (Monday):

Despite last night I felt pretty down again today. The lecture this morning was on 'The Renewing of the Mind', and it made me realize just how much junk I've got in my brain from horror movies and other such stuff that I've seen in the past. No wonder I find it hard to concentrate on God.

The evening lecture was on 'The Releasing of the Emotions', and one student jokingly passed round a box of Kleenex so that we'd be prepared for the time of prayer at the end. *I* went up for prayer afterwards, and confessed that I had a lot of bitterness inside and found it hard to express love to people. The lecturer prayed for me, then suggested that perhaps I'd built up a wall around myself that prevented me from relating to people properly. He asked me if I could remember any incident of people making fun of me at some time in the past that perhaps could have started this. I couldn't, so he just said a final general prayer for me.

I feel better after his prayer, but I honestly don't think the problem's been solved. So I have a 'wall' around myself do I? I wonder what I have to do to get rid of it?

5th June (Tuesday):

Something new today. Everyone in Holmsted Manor (students, group leaders and house staff) was split up into intercession groups that will meet three mornings a week before lectures. We start these intercession groups by asking the Lord what he wants us to pray for. Then we spend the rest of the time praying in depth for the things we feel the Lord speaking to us about (maybe praying for a particular group of people or for another country). We ended up praying for the Olympic Games in Los Angeles this morning, and I made a complete twit of myself by rebuking the power of Jesus in that area in the name of Satan. (I get very nervous and tongue-tied when I pray in public.) I hope people don't think I'm secretly a wizard or a witch or something.

In small group time we had a discussion on how we're all doing so far on the DTS. I didn't feel like talking about what happened after the lecture last night, so I just helped myself to the coffee and free Swiss chocolate while listening to everyone else. I talked to Keith privately this evening about how I've been feeling, and he was very understanding. I'm glad that he's my group leader.

6th June (Wednesday):

Instead of sitting cross-legged on the grass, I've started having my quiet times on one of the bridges over Holmsted Manor's stream. The wood smells great in the mornings, and the trickling of the water helps me feel closer to God's creation. And, more importantly, I don't get insects in my hair any more when I lie down to sleep.

A quiet day really. I was encouraged during intercession. While waiting for the Lord to speak to us, I saw a picture in my mind of a ship. I told the others in my group, and, to my surprise, someone else said he'd seen the same thing. We didn't have a clue what the relevance of a ship was, but at least I wasn't the only one making a fool of myself. Shared insanity is somehow more comforting.

These Wednesday evening drama periods are turning out to be surprisingly easy. I'm in a drama called 'The Long Silence', and all I have to do is point at the sky and shout angrily at God. Actually, I'm worried about how easy I'm finding it to be angry at God. I wonder if this means anything.

7th June (Thursday):

What a wonderful morning. I got a newspaper review of *Star Trek III* in the post from Dad, and showed it to absolutely everyone whether they wanted to see it or not (or had even *heard* of *Star Trek*). I wanted to talk about it during small group time, but everyone insisted on talking about spiritual things instead.

Before we were dismissed, we each picked the name of a fellow small group member out of an old Maxwell House coffee container. We now have to secretly pray every day for whichever name we picked. I got Keith, and I'll have to be honest, I'm not really very disciplined in my prayer times. I'll try my best to remember him, though.

8th June (Friday):

Sometime soon there's going to be a 'skit night': an evening of entertainment for the whole DTS. Every small group has to contribute at least one song or comedy sketch or something, and that was our main topic of conversation during today's small group time. It was my favourite small group time so far, and between us all we came up with quite a few interesting ideas. Unfortunately, though, they were all rejected by Keith and Laurie, so I guess we'll have to resume our planning session on Monday.

In the evening there was something called a love feast. We all had to dress up in our poshest clothes, then gather in the dining room for some really high-class food including creamy cakes. And I was in such a good mood that I actually let Laurie comb my hair the way she wants it. It's not half bad, you know!

When everything had been consumed (which didn't take very long), some of the students volunteered to stand up and tell us what they've enjoyed most about the DTS so far. One student mentioned something I found particularly interesting. She said she viewed this DTS as her second childhood, and this reminded me of our small group outing last Saturday.

I guess it's okay then for me to have fun and relax while I'm here instead of constantly analysing everything. Maybe if I don't take things so seriously, my problems will disappear (or at least shrink). I hope so. I'll start changing my attitude tomorrow.

9th June (Saturday):

So much for my change of attitude. I don't think that I've ever felt as down as I did this morning since becoming a Christian two years ago.

All of us had to go to Brighton this morning to do two open airs on the street (singing praise songs, performing dramas, and preaching). We didn't have to perform any dramas thank goodness, *or* do the preaching—that was all taken care of by members of the YWAM Brighton team. But just *being* there was bad enough. It's hard looking like a joyful Christian when there's a drunk just in front of you swearing and throwing imaginary punches, and a restless group of punks nearby who look as if they're going to start a fight at any moment. There were also a lot of bitter people in the crowd who didn't seem too appreciative of what we were doing. I don't know how on earth I'm going to cope with our three-week outreach in London.

The evening was a lot better. We played some games on the lawn, and there was also a silly costume competition. I could just about fit into my jeans so I put *them* on, and the New Zealander in our small group mascara-ed a beard and moustache on my face. The games were fun, but very exhausting.

I completely forgot about our rotten outreach this morning until I starting writing this diary entry. Oh well. These are the sacrifices a writer has to make.

10th June (Sunday):

Dad came to see me today. (He arrived in England yesterday.) He picked me up from Holmsted at 11 am, and took me to a Little Chef for a small meal with *real* pudding, including lots and lots of ice-cream! Over the meal I told him about the outreach yesterday, and he sympathized with me. Then we spent the rest of the afternoon at the house of a publishing friend where we had more *real* pudding!

It was strange being away from the DTS for a while, and quite a culture shock. I'd forgotten there was still a real world out there. It was even more of a culture shock returning to Holmsted Manor. I think I'm developing claustrophobia. We're very isolated out here, but I guess that's the idea. Less distractions from the outside world so that we can concentrate more on God.

I treated myself to a Mars bar this evening (those two puddings still hadn't filled me up), and read the last two pages of the *Star Trek III* novel that Dad brought me from America. Spock *does* come back to life. I'm so pleased. Can't wait to see the film!

11th June (Monday):

A pretty average day really.

In small group time we took turns in saying which aspect of God's character means the most to us. I said the fact that he's a friend, something I've only recently realized. And like all friendships, you have to work at it.

The main activity in the snack bar was an impromptu arm-wrestling tournament. I was enthusiastic at first, until I discovered that I'm just as bad at arm-wrestling as I appear to be at Scrabble. After my swift defeat by one of the group leader's daughters I retired to the back, cynically observing all over a can of Dr Pepper. Dr Pepper is the best drink to buy on an English DTS. All of the Europeans seem to hate it, and because there aren't many Americans here I don't have to pass the can around very often.

That *Star Trek* novel is boring. I gave up after 100 pages, and there were still 200 left to go! I hope this doesn't mean the film's going to be as bad as the last one.

12th June (Tuesday):

I woke up with a sore arm this morning. Can't think why. I prayed for it to be healed during quiet time, but nothing happened, so I rested it by falling asleep.

There was another outreach in Brighton this evening. Actually, it wasn't as bad as the last few outreaches—basically because my partner was a non-stop talker who didn't notice that I wasn't participating very much. We talked to about three people on the streets who weren't very interested, then somehow managed to bring an Indian student back to the coffee bar. He was heavily into science, which was great because it gave me the opportunity to go into long scientific arguments against evolution. I'm pretty good at logical debates. It's when I talk about my relationship with God that I don't sound quite so convincing.

13th June (Wednesday):

I was determined to learn the memory verses this morning (for a change), so I spent the whole of my quiet time marching round the grounds of Holmsted while loudly repeating 2 Corinthians 10:3–5. Other students on their quiet times didn't seem too appreciative of my enthusiastic studiousness, and the cows in the neighbouring field walked away from me. They're obviously anti-Christian cows. Just my luck, though. On the one day I actually bother to learn the verse, I'm not chosen to recite it. (Which was just as well because I'd forgotten it by the time we reached the lecture room!)

In small group time I sang the first two verses of a song I've been working on for skit night, which light-heartedly pokes fun at a few of the students. Surprisingly, Keith and Laurie actually liked it, although Keith censored verse one a bit. All I have to do now is to write a bit more, and then our small group have a song to perform on skit night.

Dad called today. I'm going to be meeting him in London on Friday so that we can drive up to Birmingham to visit some of our relatives. This means more good junk food! Hooray!

14th June (Thursday):

Today started off really well. We had an interesting conversation about dentures at the breakfast table (one of the few times I've actually managed to talk at this time in the morning), and I had a really good sleep on my bridge before intercession. But as the day unfolded I began to feel unbearably lonely, and I went for a walk to sort things out with God.

'What's wrong?' I asked him next to Holmsted's open-air swimming pool, and I felt God telling me to kneel down and dip my index finger in the water. Hoping that no one was watching, I did as I was told—and suddenly my whole perspective changed. The swimming pool was now the universe, my finger was God, and the drowing insects that were struggling on the water's surface represented the fallen human race.

When I dipped my finger inside, some of the insects raced towards me to cling on for dear life, while the others raced away, not wanting anything to do with me. None stayed in the same place. Then, almost without thinking, I pulled my finger out and deposited the rescued ants on the nearby grass while the others who had rejected me slowly drowned.

It was a wonderful picture of God's salvation, but it didn't seem to have anything to do with what I'd been praying about. God seemed to have changed the subject.

(Maybe God was right to change the subject. Maybe he was getting my mind off unimportant things, and on to things that really matter.)

15th June (Friday):

It was hard getting to sleep last night, partly through trying to figure out my experience with the swimming pool, but mainly because everyone was making animal noises in the dark. Just my rotten luck again. Just as I premiered my orang-outang impression, one of the group leaders came in to quieten us down—and I didn't realize he was in the room until he marched over to my bunk and glared at me till I stopped. Luckily no one can see you blush in the dark.

An average day really, until after work duty. I caught the train to Victoria Station, had a quarter-pounder with cheese and a chocolate milk shake at Casey Jones, then met Dad outside the station. We talked about the DTS on the way to Birmingham, and then we arrived at the house of my aunt and uncle (on

Mum's side of the family) where we had a quick cup of tea and a natter and then slept the night.

This is now my second time away from Holmsted since the start of the DTS. I wonder how I'll handle it?

16th June (Saturday):

Relatives from Liverpool drove down to see us today (on Dad's side of the family), and together we drove round different areas of Birmingham, bringing back many memories from both my and Dad's childhoods. On days like these I tend to do a lot of thinking.

For most of the two years I lived in California I was desperately homesick for England. I would scour the local bookshops and libraries for any publications that would keep me up-to-date on English goings-on, and I would faithfully see every English film that came out and every English television programme. And, if the truth be known, the main reason for me doing this DTS was that it was a good excuse for me to get back to England.

Well, here I am now back home, and am I enjoying it? Not as much as I thought I would. I wasn't a Christian the last time I was here, and today I was constantly reminded of how empty my life used to be. Yet, at the same time, I've been aware more than ever of all my shortcomings and failures as a Christian.

All day long I've had the impression that it's not my time to be out here yet . . . in the real world, that is. I've been sensing that the work God wants to do in my life is only half-complete, and that it'll be the end of the DTS before I finally feel at home again in this country. 'Yes, but there's still nine weeks left,' I complained to God, and that's almost for ever!

God was surprisingly silent today, allowing me to think through my priorities. He knows what he's doing, I keep telling myself, but somehow I don't quite believe it.

17th June (Sunday):

Dad dropped me off in London this morning before catching the next flight back to California. I wasn't in a mad rush to get back to Holmsted so I treated myself to a hamburger and went to see a film. Then I walked round London and got steadily more depressed.

For the first time ever I realized just how much this world needs God. I was totally overwhelmed by the fact that almost every person who passed me does not have that vital relationship with Jesus that we were all created for. I desperately wanted to help someone, but the need is so great. And I felt such a hypocrite as well. What right did I have to tell anyone about the joy of the Lord when I didn't have much of it myself?

The snack bar was crowded when I got back to Holmsted—a mass of chattering, laughing faces. I left before people had a chance to ask me how my weekend was, so here I am now under the stars, sitting alone on the cool grass outside while nervously crunching my Polos. I dread going up to my dormitory before 'lights out' at 11 o'clock. (Haven't I experienced this sometime before?)

18th June (Monday):

Back to the old routine, and now that I've had a short break from Holmsted I'm finding it easier to concentrate on the DTS. The two lectures this morning were especially interesting: 'Fear of the Lord' (which I honestly don't think I have) and 'Freedom From Fear'. They seem to contradict each other, don't they? But they don't really, and they gave me a lot to think about.

When I passed the kitchen this evening I accidentally heard a fellow student remarking that my clothes were 'plain and boring'. To retaliate I pinned this heartfelt appeal to the notice **board**:

Note from Andrew Wooding

I've been informed by a number of students this week that my clothes are too serious. If anyone has any 'unserious' clothes that they would like to donate to my wardrobe, please sign your name below and I will have speaks with you as soon as possible.

Thanks,

Andrew Wooding xxx

Hopefully, people will view this note as warm-hearted and refreshingly self-deprecating. Secretly I was being sarcastic.

19th June (Tuesday):

My most embarrassing quiet time ever!

While listening to a Steve Taylor tape by my bridge, I sort of got a bit carried away and started jumping up and down while pretending to play guitar. I even sang some of the songs to the disinterested cows next-door. When the tape had finished I realized that the New Zealander in our small group had been watching ten feet away for the last five minutes. 'Ulp,' was my reaction, and she gave me a pitying sort of smile before walking away without comment. It was hard getting to sleep after that.

To my surprise, quite a few people replied to yesterday's note. Here are some of their comments:

'I love you!'

'Me too!'

'"If that is how God clothes the grass of the field ...will he not much more clothe you...?" (Matthew 6:30).'

'We love you just the way you are!'

People at Holmsted know just how to encourage someone when they need it! I was blessed!

20th June (Wednesday):

Ever since I pinned that appeal to the notice board, a lot of people have been complimenting me and saying how glad they are that I'm here. I *do* appreciate their kind words, but I'm realizing more than ever just how bad I am at receiving compliments. I always feel worse after someone's been nice to me, and I don't quite know why. Maybe it's my sense of unworthiness and bad self-image. Or maybe it's just that I don't know how to respond.

There was another, not too complimentary, reply to that note today, and it was written by the person who'd originally criticized me in the kitchen: 'Stop eating Mars bars and we will find your size!' I'm not too upset with him, however, because he bought me a Mars bar a few moments ago to make up for everything. This was my first benefit from the 'Restitution' lecture we had four weeks ago. I hope *more* people criticize me!

21st June (Thursday):

Small teams were announced this morning: outreach teams that will be working in different countries from six to eight weeks, starting in September. Each team's going to be made up of about eight to ten students from this DTS plus two group leaders. The teams aren't compulsory (praise the Lord!), but we were strongly encouraged to join one—and we have the choice of three places to go to: Tanzania, Northern Ireland, or Copenhagan in Denmark.

I'm tempted to go to Denmark—it'll definitely be interesting visiting a new country—but the catch is six more weeks of that awful outreach work. We have a few days to make up our minds, but I honestly don't think I'll go.

22nd June (Friday):

My second most embarrassing quiet time!

While trying to get to sleep on my bridge, I sensed an overwhelming presence above me. At first I thought it might be God, but it turned out to be the tall Swiss chap from our dormitory. Unfortunately he had his camera with him, and he mischievously took a picture of me sprawled out on the bridge just at the moment I opened my eyes.

Somehow I'm going to have to get hold of the negative. If this picture gets to Keith and Laurie they'll probably give me a telling-off and a lecture on the importance of quiet times.

23rd June (Saturday):

My camera's on the blink. I picked up two developed rolls of film from Crawley this morning, and only the first three-and-a-half shots turned out. The last shot was a half-black close-up of my left nostril, which was obviously taken the same day I cut myself shaving. I don't know how *that* got in there!

To make up for no more photos, I treated myself to a scrapbook from W. H. Smith's so that I can at least have *some* permanent record of this DTS. I'm not exactly sure what to put in it yet, but I know I'll come up with something.

24th June (Sunday):

Another day of depression.

Church was pretty good I suppose, but unfortunately someone said something nice to me on the way back to Holmsted. Maybe I *do* give the impression on the outside of being a 'natural' and 'unpretentious' person who 'accepts everyone for who they are', but deep inside I know that's just not the case. Only I (and God) know my thoughts, and they are often *far* from accepting. And the apparent 'naturalness' is just an act. I still find it hard to express the way I really feel.

Once again I was unintentionally reminded of my inadequacies, and I tried to sleep away my depression in room 60. It's hard to wallow in self-pity, though, when your room-mates insist on having fun around you, singing and joking while mercilessly devouring coffee and chocolate digestives (which they kept trying to share with me, despite my stubborn sour expression). Very inconsiderate of them, I thought. So I transferred myself over to room 62 where the melancholy atmosphere suited my present state of mind. A lot of the chaps in there had just returned from weekends with their parents, most of whom highly disapproved of their sons going on small teams and becoming missionaries when they should really be settling down, finding good wives for themselves and getting well-paid jobs.

It was wonderful, and I had my best fit of depression since I can't remember when.

25th June (Monday):

There were two more thought-provoking lectures this morning: 'Independence' (which I'm incredibly guilty of and didn't realize was a sin until today) and 'Blood Covenant'. Then there was a small group time during which we worked on that song I've written for skit night. One of the Holmsted Manor secretaries has kindly volunteered to accompany us on the piano, so we rehearsed it with her for an hour in the lecture room. The accompaniment sounded great (much better than I thought it would), but I'm not too sure about our singing. We still have four days to work on this thing, thank goodness, and we're definitely going to need them!

I was in a good mood this evening, so I treated that New Zealander in our small group to four bags of Maltesers. She often mentions how much she likes them. There was an ulterior motive to this uncharacteristic act, however. Because there are too many for her to eat on her own, she might decide to share them in small group time tomorrow!

26th June (Tuesday):

We had Maltesers in small group time today. What a surprise! We also practised our song a few more times, then talked about the volley-ball tournament between all the small groups which starts tomorrow. Our group will be playing on Friday.

Keith and Laurie approached me afterwards to ask me if I'd like to go to Denmark with them—and before I knew it I'd said 'yes'. They said they'd pray about my decision, so *I'm* praying that the Lord will tell them I shouldn't go. It looks like I'll be doing a lot of private intercession this week.

27th June (Wednesday):

The word 'embarrassing' reached new depths for me today . . . in the swimming pool!

Laurie decided we should have small group time in the pool, but I was reluctant to join in. So, while everyone else had fun splashing around and urging me to join in every few seconds, I grumpily sat by the side, wishing for once that they'd stop being so infantile and talk about spiritual matters. Their fun was infectious, though, and after forty minutes I decided to surprise everyone by diving in with all my clothes on. Unfortunately I'd never been in the pool before, and what I thought was the deep end turned out to be dangerously shallow. The impact at the bottom didn't hurt too much, but when I emerged from the water a lot of shocked people were pointing at my bloody mouth. One of my front teeth was half missing!

The amused dentist did a great job reconstructing my tooth out of some sort of new plastic, but unfortunately it'll be too painful for me to eat for a while. It looks like I'm going to have to survive on Pot Noodles and tea sucked through a straw for the next few days.

Praise God that nothing worse happened to me in the pool.

28th June (Thursday):

I don't know how many times so far I've had to tell people what happened to my tooth. I've never found it easy to be the centre of attention, especially when it's for something like this. After dinner I poured out my heart to Keith about this, and also about me finding it hard when people are nice to me. We sort of came to the conclusion that a lot of my emotions were blocked, although we weren't sure why.

While singing 'I Love You Lord' during praise and worship this evening, the Lord very clearly told me that I *didn't* love him. This crushed me, and I sat down in shame, not quite sure how to pray. Every word of the 'Compassion' lecture that followed seemed to be aimed right at me. I realized just how much I'd hardened my heart over the years (I was unable to love God properly, and found it hard to love my fellow human beings as well), and I also remembered what I was told three weeks ago about that 'wall' I'd built around myself after people making fun of me.

I went over to two of the group leaders afterwards and told them about this 'wall'. At their advice I forgave those people who made fun of me (whoever they were), repented of my lack of compassion, told God how much I love him, and then the group leaders prayed for me. At first I was tense while they were praying, but soon the tension disappeared and it was replaced by a wonderful sense of peace and relief.

I praise God for what happened tonight. My bitterness seems to have gone, and I also feel a new love for God. Maybe I'll now find it easier to relate to people. I hope so.

29th June (Friday):

Remember I 'felt' a few weeks ago that our small group would win the volley-ball tournament? Well, I guess I'm not a prophet. Our team got thrashed after just five minutes, so they spent the rest of small group time trying to find my tooth at the bottom of the pool. I didn't particularly want to relive my traumatic experience, so I decided not to join in.

Skit night in the barn was brill: over two-and-a-half hours of comedy sketches, songs and monologues from the students, leaders and house staff. There are a lot of talented people here. We performed *our* song just before the intermission, and it was received surprisingly well. People kept coming up to me afterwards to say how good they thought it was. Something *did* happen last night—I actually enjoyed their compliments!

Now that I'm more mature in my walk with the Lord, I've decided to start growing a moustache.

30th June (Saturday):

I left Holmsted again this weekend, this time to visit Walton-on-Thames where I lived for ten years before moving to California in the summer of '82. It was strange being back. So much has happened to me during the DTS, and yet here I was with mostly non-Christian friends who've been living their lives as usual these last few weeks without the slightest idea of all the things I've been experiencing, or even that those sorts of things can actually happen. I tried to tell them what I'd been up to, but most of them seemed more interested in earthbound matters.

I visited some friends of our family in the evening, who let me drive up to London with them to hear Luis Palau at Queens Park Rangers Stadium. Only one of them is a Christian, so naturally I spent the whole of Luis's sermon praying for their salvation. Unfortunately none of them went forward to get saved, and the message fell on apparently deaf ears.

I'm disillusioned with England. No one's interested in God. No one. I'm dreading our three-week outreach in London.

1st July (Sunday):

Well, a peaceful weekend, despite yesterday's disappointments. And I did some more reflecting as I walked round London.

I definitely feel a lot better about myself since that 'Compassion' lecture, and I think I understand why. When those people made fun of me I must have become very self-conscious, not expressing my *real* feelings for fear of being made fun of again. I guess that's one of the reasons I've been finding street work so hard: fear of ridicule. I'm going to have to work on expressing myself more now, and with so many understanding people around me at Holmsted, that won't be too difficult.

I got back to the dormitory after 'lights out' (I'm writing this by torchlight under my blankets), and discovered a note on my bunk. The note read: 'Andrew, we have been missing you a lot,' and it was signed by everyone in the dorm. This is definitely going in my scrapbook!

It's good to be back.

2nd July (Monday):

During our lecture on 'The Kingdom of God' this evening, the lecturer told us how he met his wife. Apparently they were both students on the same YWAM School of Evangelism, and the lecturer was in charge of the snack bar. When his wife-to-be fell ill, the lecturer took it upon himself to hand-feed her yoghurt in her room every day. Needless to say, it was during these times together that they discovered how much they liked each other.

After the lecture the girl from *our* snack bar came up to me and said: 'You'll have to buy *me* some yoghurt, Andrew!' I wasn't quite sure how to reply. No one's ever said anything like that to me before.

3rd July (Tuesday):

Our small group went to a nearby restaurant this evening for a special birthday meal. Two of us have birthdays tomorrow (including me), and it's Keith's birthday today. So we sort of killed three birds with one stone—chicken in *my* case, and then some ice-cream.

There were two additions to my scrapbook when we got back to Holmsted: a chap from room 62 volunteered to sketch a profile of me (which turned out quite well), and that New Zealander in our small group donated a squashed Malteser. It took us ages to sello-tape it down! I've now only got forty-five more pages to fill.

4th July (Wednesday):

Our small group sat together in the dining room today to celebrate our two birthdays (which meant two whole birthday cakes!). *My* cake looked exactly like a Birds custard container, but it didn't look that way for long!

There was also an American Independence Day celebration outside the barn for all the Americans at Holmsted, and I was allowed to join them since I've been living in America for a while. Halfway through the celebration, a gang of English YWAMers dressed as Red Indians (or pale white Indians!) barged in, looking very menacing and obviously quite miffed at not being asked to participate in the festivities. But we soon discovered to our relief that they were on a peace-keeping mission. The Indian Chief announced his intentions to 'transform Anglo-American relations previously severed due to tea', poured a cuppa for the leader of YWAM England (an American), then left with the others, never to be seen by us again. Luckily they didn't steal any of our hamburgers, which meant I could have seconds.

I got a whole pile of birthday cards today, a lot of them from California. Receiving these brought back memories of America—especially of my family—and I felt bad about how rotten I've been to my parents and younger brother in the past. I wrote a letter to them all this evening, asking for their forgiveness.

5th July (Thursday):

A lot of people have been coming up to me these last few days, expressing their surprise at how young I am. Apparently many people thought I was five or more years older. I've also discovered that I'm not the youngest person on this DTS—far from it! It was stupid of me to feel inferior about my age at the beginning. People here accept you no matter what age you are.

I am now twenty years old, but I still can't grow a moustache. It's been almost a week since I started now, and the only things I can see under my nose are the two red spots where I cut myself shaving.

6th July (Friday):

Everyone on the DTS went up to London this evening, both for outreach work and also for intercession for our three weeks there. I was paired off with Laurie again to walk the streets, and despite her constant encouragement I still found it hard to witness to people.

Afterwards we all met up in a Christian coffee bar opposite Victoria coach station. We had a short praise and worship session, then were split up into our small groups to pray for London for an hour. Surprisingly, I saw a picture in my mind while praying. I saw God standing in a field of broken flowers. He was crying because he cared so much for those flowers, and one by one he was stooping down and mending them. The flowers obviously represented the broken people of London that God wants to heal both physically and spiritually, and he was promising to heal many of them during our outreach.

I was so tired when I got back to Holmsted that I'm writing this tomorrow morning. I really enjoyed myself last night (in spite of my failures on the streets), and it was good being back in a city again.

7th July (Saturday):

There was a wedding reception at Holmsted today for two former students, and I was in charge of carrying all the sound equipment outside. It was hard work lugging around those heavy loudspeakers and all the other stuff, and when the reception had finished I had to take them all back to the tape department again. Naturally, I was shattered after all this work and also very hungry, so I staggered along to the kitchen to see if there were any leftovers from the reception feast. This was a terrible mistake since I got roped into helping with the washing-up—and I was in there for a whole two hours!

Getting married isn't as hard as people make it out to be. Everyone else does the work for you!

8th July (Sunday):

It was quiet around Holmsted today. Most people were recovering from yesterday's wedding reception, including me.

In the evening I played Scrabble again with that girl from the snack bar. (She won, as usual.) After the game she asked me: 'Andrew, do you ever have any problems? You always seem so cheerful.' At first I wondered how she could possibly have missed all my trials and tribulations during the DTS, especially since she's in the same small group. But then it occurred to me that I haven't really been very open about what I've been going through, stubbornly trying to sort out my problems for myself—and there's only so much you can sort out on your own.

I've been open with you, dear diary, haven't I? And I guess I'm open with God as well. But being open with other people. Now that's a different matter....

9th July (Monday):

The dining area was surprisingly alive with conversation this morning. All the teddy bears in Holmsted Manor mysteriously disappeared last night, and people were loudly theorizing over their muesli or cornflakes what might have happened to them. One student was so stricken with grief that he requested a leave of absence for two days to recover. Needless to say, he was turned down. It was a good try, though!

We were given a short briefing on the London outreach before this evening's lecture, and were told where we're going to be working. We've been split up into three teams—the Victoria team, the Earl's Court team, and the Leicester Square and Covent Garden team. I'm in the Victoria team which is just as bad as any other area I suppose. You can tell I'm not looking forward to this outreach!

10th July (Tuesday):

Our small group went on a picnic this lunchtime with the group led by Per Eivind and Ellinor Stig, a Norwegian couple who are going to be starting a YWAM base in Denmark next year. Naturally, Keith and Laurie spent a lot of time asking them questions about Copenhagen so that they'll know what to expect when they lead the small team.

Afterwards, Keith and Laurie congratulated me on the fact that I'll be going to Copenhagen with them. It was hard trying to look pleased at this—mainly because I wasn't. Six weeks of outreach work doesn't exactly fit my definition of fun.

I guess I'd better write to my parents again to tell them I won't be coming home for a while.

11th July (Wednesday):

I discovered today how long it took one of our small group members to bake that birthday cake for me. She gave up three hours of her valuable time . . . just for *me*! I almost choked when I heard this, and I guess I still haven't completely got used to people being kind to me. I went up to one of the leaders afterwards, and asked him to pray with me about this. His prayer really blessed me, even though he kept referring to me as 'John' instead of 'Andrew'. I've obviously made a great impression on the leaders of this school.

We had to perform all our dramas and dances in front of each other in drama period this evening— which was quite nerve-wracking. And it's especially hard trying to look angry when three people on the front row are pulling funny faces at you! I don't know how I'm going to cope with doing this drama in London every day.

I'm going to have to cut down on food again. I'm rapidly putting on weight.

12th July (Thursday):

We passed photographs round in small group time today, and the most popular one seemed to be that shot of my nose! Then we sat in a circle and prayed for each other.

I'm going to miss this small group when the DTS has finished. Although we've only known each other a few weeks, we've grown extraordinarily close. I'm going to miss this DTS as well. It's been tough a lot of the time, but worth every second of it. I can now say with some conviction that I finally have a meaningful relationship with God, although I still have a lot to learn.

The plot thickens. One student found a leg from his teddy bear in his cornflakes this morning, and there was an anonymous message on the lecture room's blackboard which read: 'You'll Never See Them Again!'

Speaking of not seeing things, there's still no sign of my moustache.

13th July (Friday):

Our lecture this morning was about 'How to Give Testimonies on Outreach'. Apparently each one of us will have to speak on how we became Christians for at least one open air in London, which I'm really not too thrilled about since I get very nervous when speaking in public. I've been practising how to look feverish at a moment's notice, so that I'll have an excuse when the leaders pick on me during the outreach!

We had our second love feast tonight, which was great fun and a lot more informal than the last time—

probably because we students are now more relaxed. First we sat in different groups in the barn, chomping on hamburgers and telling jokes about the DTS. And then we played some energetic party games to burn off the food. I haven't laughed so much in ages! I went for a short walk afterwards to thank God for all the fun I was having, and his Holy Spirit filled me with so much joy that it was almost too hard to take.

God is so good to me. I honestly don't know why.

14th July (Saturday):

We did two more open airs in Brighton this morning, and had to perform all our dances and dramas (including 'The Long Silence'). Both open airs went surprisingly well, and, to my amazement, I didn't get nervous once. Afterwards our small group went for fish and chips, which I really enjoyed (especially the milk shake I drank with it).

It was talent night in the evening (similar to skit night except that we didn't have to be funny). My contribution was a song about cows, which people seemed to like even though I have a dreadful singing voice. But the highlight was a mock rock group (comprised mostly of students from room 62) miming to 'Why Should the Devil Have All the Good Music' by Cliff Richard. It was absolutely hilarious, especially that part where the tape broke down! I wonder if they planned it that way?

I've started eating Spangles instead of Mars bars, so hopefully I'll now lose weight.

15th July (Sunday):

All of the guys in our dormitory had a get-together in the reading room this evening. First we ate something called Swiss fondue (which was scrumptious), and then we sat in a circle and shared what we appreciated most about each other. Their comments about me were very touching, though at times I found it hard to believe that they were actually talking about *me*.

After we'd finished, I received a telephone call from a friend in Walton-on-Thames (one of the people I went to see Luis Palau with two weekends ago). At first I thought that something was wrong, and that she was calling to say there'd been a death in my family or something. But she quickly proved me wrong. 'Andrew,' she said, 'I just thought I'd call to tell you I've become a Christian.' The four of them had gone to see Luis Palau again on the closing night of his Mission to London, she told me, and all three non-Christians went forward to give their lives to the Lord.

I couldn't speak for the rest of the call because I was crying so much...and I'm still crying now. I'm sensing God's joy for these people and their new life in Jesus, and can almost hear the rejoicing in heaven (see Luke 15:7).

I forgot my Spangles arrangement in all the excitement, and bought myself a Mars bar. But I don't mind. That sort of thing doesn't seem to matter at the moment. So people in England *are* interested in God.

16th July (Monday):

I don't believe it. There are only three days of lectures left. This DTS has flown by!

The lectures this morning were on 'Apologetics': how to logically defend the Christian faith to people we speak to on the streets. Absolutely fascinating, and I took tons of notes which is a sure sign that I was enjoying myself. I practised what we'd learnt on the cows during lunch, but they obviously needed time to think about what I'd told them.

The mystery of the missing teddy bears still hasn't been solved. That student found another leg in his cornflakes this morning, and there was a chalk outline in the shape of a teddy bear corpse at the foot of the hallway stairs. If the teddy bears don't turn up soon, there's going to be a mock funeral for them outside the barn.

17th July (Tuesday):

Laurie snipped my locks again today, which was very kind of her, although I still had to put up with her complaints that my hair is too old-fashioned. Then I met with her and Keith for another one of our private sessions, and we had a good natter about the DTS, and also about the Copenhagen small team. Keith told me that he made a vow at the beginning of the DTS not to eat chocolate bars or anything else from the snack bar unless people buy them for him. I admire his faith.

Spangles just don't compare with Mars bars I'm afraid, so I guess I'm going to have to lose weight some other way.

18th July (Wednesday):

We had to reveal today which small group member we're supposed to have been praying for, and I sheepishly admitted to Keith that I haven't been too faithful in praying for him. 'No wonder I've been having so many problems recently,' he told me, and I started feeling guilty. But then he let me have some of his chocolate digestives, so we're obviously still friends. Our small group won't meet together now until after the London outreach.

There was a communion service in the dining room this evening for everyone in Holmsted Manor. It was marvellous, especially since we now all feel so close. Then we students had to transport all our stuff outside to the main field. From now on we're going to be sleeping in tents so that our dormitories can be tidied for the next DTS.

All the teddy bears reappeared by their owners' beds last night. No one's quite sure who the thief was, but that girl who works in the nursery looks incredibly guilty whenever it's mentioned.

19th July (Thursday):

A summer camp is going to be held on the grounds of Holmsted next week—like a sort of mini-DTS with worship, teaching and ministry times. Over 300 people are expected to attend (not including students), and many of them are going to be joining us on the London outreach.

The camp starts on Monday, so, after the dormitories have been cleaned, most of the students have got the next few days off—except for me, still faithfully plugging away in the tape department. There's going to be a big demand for tapes during the camp, so I'll be under quite a lot of pressure. On top of that, I discovered today that I'm going to have to co-lead a small group on the camp with a YWAMer from the London base. I'm not that worried, though. If it's anything like *our* small group, it'll be a lot of fun.

It was hard getting to sleep last night, especially since all the male students are now together in one large tent. To celebrate our first night outside, the boys from room 60 tried to impress the others with their animal impressions. Needless to say, room 62 joined in. I didn't participate myself since I didn't want to get told off again. Instead I quietly rolled over in my sleeping bag and did a highly convincing impression of a bear in hibernation.

20th July (Friday):

Everyone from Holmsted gathered outside on the lawn this afternoon so that a photograph of the whole DTS could be taken. Actually about fifty photographs, since nearly every student and group leader wanted a shot taken with their own camera. This meant that we were outside for over half an hour, and it was quite exhausting having to smile for each picture.

I predict that these photos will becomes collector's items, since it'll probably be the last time I pose without a moustache. Although the moustache doesn't seem to be growing yet, my faith *is* growing—and that's what counts!

Sound really travels in this field at night. Although the girls' tent is quite far away from us, we can hear them doing *their* own animal impressions very clearly.

The females on this DTS are a lot more talented than I'd thought!

21st July (Saturday):

Everything we do seems to be outside nowadays, and I'm starting to develop agoraphobia. We eat outside, play outside, wash outside using the sinks next to the barn...and although we don't shower or go to the toilet outside, we have to now use the facilities by the garages which means a long walk *outside*. I mentioned my problem to the cook, and she was far from sympathetic. She told me, 'If you're so desperate to escape the outdoors, you can stay in the kitchen and peel potatoes for the summer camp.' Keith and a Swiss chap helped me and it took us almost three hours to get through the allotted amount of spuds. I was so thirsty afterwards that I bought myself a Dr Pepper from the snack bar, which is now in the barn. Unfortunately the snack bar closed just after my purchase, so I had to drink it... outside!

There was a review of *Star Trek III* in the *Daily Telegraph* today, which means it has at last been released in England. There are lots of cinemas in London, so now I have a reason to look forward to the three-week outreach!

22nd July (Sunday):

Today was our last day together as a DTS for a while, before all those intruders arrive for the summer camp and before we're split up for the London outreach. It's pretty sad really.

Some of the summer camp participants arrived

today, so lots of new tents have sprouted up all over the field. Our leader has informed us that from now on the boys' and girls' tents are going to have to remain quiet in the evenings so that we don't disturb anyone. There was some grumbling when this was announced, but I'm quite pleased. It normally takes me a while to get to sleep every night, and horses neighing and pigs going 'oink' hardly helps.

For a change, I'm not eating anything while writing this. The smell of cows from the field next to this tent has somehow ruined my appetite.

23rd July (Monday):

I have mixed feelings about this summer camp.

My job today was to guide incoming cars to the parking area, and it was quite exciting at first seeing everyone arriving. My excitement waned, however, when we queued up outside for the evening meal and I was suddenly surrounded by hundreds of strange new people. It was just like the start of the DTS, and my old paranoia and sense of inferiority returned. I walked over to my quiet-time bridge afterwards so that I could pray, but I was beaten there by a couple of the intruders.

I resent these people breaking up our close-knit DTS. Don't they know we've been here a whole eleven weeks, and gone through a lot together? After just a few hours at Holmsted, they think they can trample all over the grounds as if they own the place.

There was an introductory meeting this evening in a large tent that's been put up in the garden area. I have to admit that praise and worship with about 400 people was quite exhilarating, but my mind wandered a lot during the teaching on 'Revival'. And the snack bar afterwards was utter chaos. I didn't feel like standing in another queue full of strangers, so I returned to the boys' tent to write this diary entry.

Maybe I'll feel more at ease with these people when I start to lead a group tomorrow.

24th July (Tuesday):

Group leading. Ugh.

After a morning meeting in the big tent and then a choice of different lectures (I went to the 'Healing' one), all the small group leaders had to meet in the dining area for a short time of prayer and encouragement. As well as leading our small group every day, my co-leader and I are going to have to meet individually with each member at least once during the week for a counselling session. How on earth am I going to find the time?

Our small group is comprised entirely of intruders, and our first meeting together was a disaster. Luckily, I'm only the assistant leader so I didn't have to do that much talking, but I still felt very intimidated. The average age seems to be twenty-four, and all have at least a college education—while I'm merely a twenty-year-old who never made it past four miserable 'O' levels. Sue was the main group leader, and she performed admirably, considering the fact that most of the group seemed reluctant to talk. There were a lot of embarrassed silences during that first period, and I was the one getting embarrassed.

I didn't get my daily dose of chocolate tonight because the snack bar was busy again. This week's going to last for ever.

25th July (Wednesday):

I didn't have to co-lead the small group today, praise God. I volunteered to help clean the building in Bermondsey that the Victoria team are going to be sleeping in, and our cleaning duties just happened to coincide with small group period. I don't normally volunteer for things like this, but I felt unusually charitable today. I wonder why?

We got back just in time for the evening meal, so I patiently waited in line for my helping, then tried to find someone on the field to sit next to. No luck, I'm afraid. All my student friends were eating with members of their small groups, combining meal-time with their counselling sessions. I didn't want to barge in on their private conversations, and I didn't feel up to socializing with the intruders either—so I retired to the privacy of the tape department where I ate my spaghetti in solitude, feeling thoroughly rejected.

It rained terribly last night. The students' tents held up well, thank goodness, but the tents of most of the intruders either flooded or collapsed. I was really pleased about that.

26th July (Thursday):

Group leading again. And Sue wants me to be the main leader tomorrow, which means *I* now have to do most of the talking. What on earth am I going to say? I worried about this in the tape department for most of the rest of the day. (People have started ordering tapes, which means I'll now be busy in there for the rest of the camp.)

I found a Mars bar on my sleeping bag when I

returned to the tent a few minutes ago. I haven't a clue who it's from, but it really cheered me up.

Then I remembered about small group period tomorrow, so now I'm depressed again.

27th July (Friday):

I told Keith and Laurie this morning how I was feeling about group leading—about all my fears and my sense of inadequacy. Both listened patiently to my rantings, and then kindly prayed for me. Afterwards Laurie calmly reassured me that there was no need to worry. 'Just be yourself in the small group,' she advised. 'Be natural, and God will bless that. There's nothing else you can do.'

Good advice, I thought, so I started today's small group period by recounting in detail all my difficulties during the DTS, and how God had blessed me so much despite my spiritual immaturity. To my surprise, I couldn't shut the group up for the rest of the period, and there were *no* embarrassing silences. My honesty seemed to open everyone up, and people were falling over themselves to share secrets from their past and how God has been working in their lives.

I'm not ging to call these people 'intruders' any more. They have their problems like everyone else, and have just as much of a thirst for God as we students—and God loves us all equally. To make up for my bad attitude, I bought ten Mars bar this evening to give away in tomorrow's small group period. (Actually I bought eleven Mars bars, but one of them's now in my tummy!)

28th July (Saturday):

It was a nightmare in the tape department this morning. One of the duplicating machines broke down, which means it'll take me almost twice as long to get everyone's tapes ready before leaving for London on Monday. From now on I'll have to spend every spare moment down there, and even then I doubt if I'll be able to finish them all in time.

I related my panic to Sue and the small group today, and they were very understanding. They even said they didn't mind me not having the time for individual counselling sessions. (I think those Mars bars had something to do with them not being too harsh on me.) Anyway, guess where I spent the rest of the afternoon. Correct first time. I'm so glad it doesn't smell in there any more.

The different teams going to London were announced tonight. There's about seventy in *our* team: one-third DTS students, and two-thirds intru...I mean, summer camp people. All of us met together briefly to pray for our work in Victoria, and then I rushed back to the tape department for another hour of hard slog. Praise God that the duplicating machine broke down. Now I don't have to counsel anyone (Romans 8:28).

It's quiet in the tent as I write this. Believe it or not, I actually miss those animal noises!

29th July (Sunday):

There was a beautiful worship service in the main tent this morning, and it concluded with communion. Then the summer camp officially finished, and those not going to London tomorrow were allowed to leave. *I* wasn't, worst luck, so I quickly did some laundry and then spent the rest of the day trying not to say nasty things to the broken-down duplicating machine. Before returning to the tent tonight, I took my clothes down from the washing line by the faint light of my torch. (I must buy some new batteries for that thing.)

I'll be dreaming about tapes tonight. I duplicated so many today, and there are still tons more to be done. I'm going to have to wake up early tomorrow to get them all finished before London.

30th July (Monday):

Praise God for a miracle this morning. I prayed for the duplicating machine to be healed, and, sure enough, it started to copy tapes perfectly—much to my surprise! Just over three hours later I rushed the completed tapes to the main office to be mailed out, breathlessly retrieved my bags from the boys' tent, and then ran puffing and sweating to the coach just ten minutes before it was due to leave for London. Once inside, I collapsed into the nearest vacant seat, ready for a good sleep. Unfortunately, though, it was only mid-day, and it would be another ten hours before I'd get my well-earned kip. Until then I had to do an Oscar-deserving performance of pretending to be awake.

The rest of the day we tidied up the building in Bermondsey a bit more, rehearsed a few new dramas (which unfortunately I've got to be in), figured out where we'd all be sleeping (there are two large halls—one for boys and one for girls), and then we gathered in the meeting room upstairs so that our leaders could explain the daily routine to us.

Keith and Laurie are sadly not on the Victoria team, but most of the rest of our small group are. That's small consolation, though, for having to do three weeks of street work. Hopefully our time in London will go quickly.

31st July (Tuesday):

I was miserable most of the morning because I didn't sleep much last night. Then at 12 pm I was handed some gooey green stuff in a bowl which someone informed me was lunch. That did nothing to cheer me up. And afterwards there was another meeting upstairs which was supposed to fire our enthusiasm for today's street work. Unfortunately it's hard to fire up something that's non-existent.

I wasn't scared on the streets today—just sort of apathetic. And as soon as I could, I ducked into the nearest McDonald's for some *real* food. That gooey green stuff and the packed lunch we were given (two sandwiches, a bag of Smith's crips, and a French Golden Delicious) failed to fill me up. I didn't witness to anyone in the coffee bar this evening—just cracked jokes with a few fellow team-members who seemed like-minded.

To my horror, I discovered when we got back to Bermondsey that I had only brought one pair of socks with me—the ones I'm wearing now. I must have left the others on Holmsted's washing line when taking my clothes down in the dark the other night. One crisis after another—this seems to be the life of a true Christian disciple. I'm going to be mature about this, however. I consider it pure joy, dear diary, because the loss of my socks will test my faith and develop perseverance in me (James 1:2).

I won't half pong, though.

1st August (Wednesday):

Getting showered every day is going to be interesting. We have to wash at Lambeth Baths, which means a twenty-minute walk to the bus stop, a wait for the bus both ways, and then another twenty-minute walk back to the base. And in this dirty London air, we're just as much in need of a shower when we return as when we leave! Today was quite fun, though. I opted for a bath instead of a shower, and read an article about *Star Trek III* while soaking in the tub.

I had to be in two dramas today: 'Hands', a short retelling of the gospel story, and 'The Chicken Sketch' in which we pretend to be chickens, jet aeroplanes and maniacal monkeys. Great fun, and at last I can get away with my animal noises! I still didn't speak to anyone on the street, though. I didn't see the point.

I severely injured one of my fingers while trying to cut open a custard carton tonight. Serves me right for being greedy, I suppose. While eating it, I witnessed to the two hamsters in the food storage room to ease my guilt about being so apathetic. They weren't too interested in the gospel, but they loved the custard I gave them.

Like me, I think they're going to have to get their priorities sorted out.

2nd August (Thursday):

We didn't have to do any dramas today. One of the permanent London YWAM teams performed a half-hour musical in Sloane Square, and all *we* had to do was hand out tracts and witness to people afterwards.

While disinterestedly doling the tracts out, I noticed one of our team-members witnessing to someone. To my surprise, she actually looked like she was enjoying herself, and there was a lot of that joy of the Lord in her face. It occurred to me then that witnessing might actually be fun, so I repented of my bad attitude and marched over to the nearest stranger to give him my testimony. He was very open to what I was saying, but after two minutes he sheepishly admitted that he was actually a member of our team, someone I hadn't noticed before. I was ever so embarrassed.

I witnessed to a lot of people today. It's exhausting, but also invigorating at the same time, and, if nothing else, it's strengthened my faith. The hamsters haven't made a commitment yet, but I'm still working on them. I'm believing for their salvation by the end of the outreach.

3rd August (Friday):

I felt sorry for our dancing team today. The sound system started acting up during our second open air, and the song they were dancing to got steadily slower and slower. They bravely continued, however, and their well-choreographed routine lasted twice as long as it should have (although to them it must have seemed even longer!). The open air wasn't a total failure, though. As a result of the dance we got about three times as many people as normal stopping to watch us, and I think a couple of them even got saved.

I couldn't find my towel when I got back to the base and I suspected foul play, so I put this announcement up on the notice board:

> If anyone has any clues as to the whereabouts of Andrew
> Wooding's towel, could you please see him immediately?
> Also, information is needed regarding the identity of the
> thief. Andrew will only get slightly angry with the culprit,
> and promises not to do anything in revenge at all. The
> reward is two Smarties.

4th August (Saturday):

A few punk rockers were among those watching our
open air this afternoon, and they really seemed to
enjoy it, especially 'The Chicken Sketch'. Afterwards
one of them showed me a trick she could do with the
mouse that lives in her hair. She dropped it in her
mouth and closed it so that just the tail could be seen,
thrashing backwards and forwards between her lips.
Then she handed the mouse to her boyfriend who did
exactly the same thing. As much as I like these people,
I hope no one invites them back to our base. I'm
concerned for the safety of my hamsters.

Some joker has altered my announcement. Instead
of 'towel' it now says 'brain', and this reply was pinned
below it:

> Found! One brain belonging to Andrew Wooding. Note
> the symmetry of the organ. This disc shape should slide
> in where the other fell out. I'll accept the Smarties when
> you have them!

Taped to the reply was a green Refresher which I
presume was supposed to be my brain. Very funny, I
don't think!

I found my towel at the top of my clothes' bag this

evening. I didn't think to look there yesterday. Oops.

5th August (Sunday):

After church this morning we had to do some door-to-door evangelism: knocking on doors and witnessing to people. The block of flats my partner and I were assigned to was very unresponsive to the gospel, which was bad in a way, I suppose, but also good because we were finished sooner than we expected and had more free time.

The first lady we talked to almost immediately slammed her door in our faces. 'I don't want to hear about your Christianity,' she screamed at us. 'I've got my own religion. I'm a Catholic.' *Slam!*

The second lady was equally as impolite. 'I'm not interested in Christ. I go to Westminster Abbey every week.' *Slam!*

And so it was for most of the rest of the block. The only decent conversations we had were with a Jew on the second floor, and a Hindu lady on the third. For some reason, they were more interested in what we had to say than the 'Christians'.

Before our open airs tonight, I went to see the last half hour of *Star Trek III* and the first ten minutes. Absolutely triff! I can't wait to see it all the way through!

6th August (Monday):

Our first free day today, and after a whole week of exhausting outreach work it was definitely needed. First, all the DTS students from the different teams met together in Regent's Park for some sandwiches and to catch up on each other's news. Then we trekked over to St Paul's Cathedral for a quick look round, and after just an hour there (old churches are really boring) I trekked over to the Plaza, Piccadilly Circus, to finally experience the full-length version of *Star Trek III: The Search for Spock*. What can I say? Probably the best film I've seen this year. It was *that* good.

I realized while eating fish and chips this afternoon that I finally feel at home in England. Praise God for days like these. I praise him for all the new friends he's given me, and also for the peace I feel. And I especially praise him for real English fish and chips!

Now I've got to wait another three years to see the next *Star Trek* film. Oh well.

7th August (Tuesday):

There's nothing in the world like an open air. First, ten minutes of exhilarating praise and worship (no matter how many of the spectators are making fun of us, I just keep my eyes on God), then a few dramas and testimonies, and then the preaching during which we spread out among the crowd and talk to them individually about Christ. A number of people we've spoken to have become Christians so far and we've even seen people being healed on the street!

Instead of travelling on the underground, a few of us took the bus back to Bermondsey this evening. It was incredible. London looks spectacular at night, especially the Thames. I'm so glad the Lord has brought me back to England. I never want to leave.

8th August (Wednesday):

Another good day on the streets, and in the evening our team had a love feast in the coffee bar: hamburgers and potato salad, and then a talent competition. *My* talent was the hit of the evening, although I'm not quite sure why. I thought *everyone* could ripple their stomach.

There was a squelching sound when I sat on my sleeping bag to write this diary entry. Curious, I unzipped it and found inside a squashed banana, a scrubbing brush, and about 3,000,000 cornflakes. I wasn't sure who was responsible, so again I had to make use of the notice board:

> For the person who put ground cornflakes, a squashed banana and a scrubbing brush in my sleeping bag: Psalm 28:3–4.
> Much love,
> Andrew Wooding xxx

My socks are driving me crazy. As soon as I can, I'm going to get them washed.

9th August (Thursday):

All three London teams met together in a church in Earl's Court this afternoon for a worship meeting, and also to find out how we've all been doing. It was quite enjoyable really, except that I fell asleep during the sermon, much to my embarrassment. You know, I didn't realize I snored.

Afterwards, all the Denmark team had to meet outside for a short update on our outreach. It was good to see Keith and Laurie again, and if our time in Denmark is half as enjoyable as *this* outreach then it's going to be great.

While writing this, an electronic alarm clock went off in the boys' hall and persistently kept beeping for about five minutes. 'I wish someone would turn that thing off,' I kept thinking. 'Don't they know I'm trying to concentrate?' Then it occurred to me that the beeping might be nearer than I thought, and, sure enough, a quick search revealed the offending timepiece at the bottom of my sleeping bag.

Obviously this prank was perpetrated by the same person who gave me breakfast in bed last night. I'm going to have to do some investigating.

10th August (Friday):

The London premiere of 'The Long Silence'—the one drama we spent the whole of the DTS rehearsing—was, to put it mildly, a disaster. One of our 'thespians' was busy witnessing to some Muslims, and didn't realize we'd actually *started* the drama until being pulled away by the scruff of his neck by another leading player. It was hard looking angry at God after that, and 'The Long Giggle' would be a more accurate title of how the drama ended up. At least it made a change from 'Hands' and 'The Chicken Sketch'.

A reliable source informed me today that it was that girl from Holmsted's snack bar who sabotaged my sleeping bag last week. Ignoring Hebrew's 10:30, I secretly wrapped her *Anne of Green Gables* book with cling film, dropped it in a see-through plastic bag, then put it in another see-through plastic bag full of water. Then I left the whole package in the freezer, ready for her to find the next day.

I can't wait to see her reaction!

11th August (Saturday):

To give me a bit of a break from street work, I've volunteered to help out with a children's club next week that's going to be held each afternoon in a nearby church. I met with some of the other volunteers today for a quick time of prayer, and then we distributed leaflets about the club in the neighbourhood. Each day we're going to perform dramas for the kids, play new games with them, and hopefully lead a few of them to the Lord as well. I'm in charge of giving them memory verses each day, which means I can take out on the kiddywinks all the frustration I felt at *Keith's* memory verses. Aren't I rotten!

I went to the launderette this morning, but forgot to put my socks in the machine with the rest of my clothes. Luckily they don't pong *that* much at the moment, but after another few days of outreach...who knows?

12th August (Sunday):

Peter, my younger brother, arrived in England today for a two-week holiday. He wanted to see what I'm up to in London, so I met him outside Victoria Station and took him to the coffee bar (with a short stop on the way in McDonald's). Peter was impressed with what he saw (with the coffee bar, that is—*not* the McDonald's!), and he's promised to see me again on Wednesday.

There was some commotion when I got back to the

base. Someone had let the hamsters loose in the men's hall, and people were running all over the place, frantically trying to retrieve them. For animals that look tired all the time, they sure run fast!

13th August (Monday):

The first day of our children's club was fun, even though we didn't get quite the turn-out we'd expected. There were only five children to *eight* of us supervisors! Still, I enjoyed guzzling down the refreshments when no one else was looking. And one of the six-year-olds kindly showed me how to do foot painting with pink paint. It took me ages to get the mess off the church floor when we'd finished.

We had to perform 'Hands' yet again tonight— twice! I'm getting fed up with 'Hands', even though it's always very effective. In the coffee bar I secretly wrote a joke version of it called 'Socks', and showed it to my fellow actors. All of them loved it, and we're thinking of premiering it at our second love feast on Wednesday.

It's funny, you know. My socks now smell like paint.

14th August (Tuesday):

Our cook found *Anne of Green Gables* today. She spotted an extra block of ice in the freezer and thought, 'Great. More meat to feed the starving hordes.' (If only it *was* more meat!) As soon as she realized she'd been had, she promptly returned it to its rightful owner who left it by the radiator to thaw out. I think that girl from the snack bar enjoyed the joke, but the cook's only comment to me was: 'Don't waste our plastic bags in future.' It looks like my attempt to preserve this great work of literature was met with a cool reception. (Pause for laughter.)

The cook also informed me that the hamsters have now been taken to a safer place (away from the base and out of reach of us men). I am overcome with grief since I'll probably never see them again.

There was a bigger turn-out at the children's club today. That six-year-old brought along her younger brother.

15th August (Wednesday):

It was hard for me to witness to people today. I woke up with a terrible earache this morning, and also lots of thoughts of worthlessness and inadequacy. I know that this is probably Satan trying to bring me down (I'm especially susceptible to his lies when I'm exhausted), but sometimes it's hard to shake off thoughts like these.

Our second open air helped me forget about my earache for a few minutes. While one of my Norwegian friends was trying to give his testimony, a policeman barged in on us and insisted on seeing our permit. He was convinced we were breaking the law, and for one wonderful moment I thought we were all going to be arrested—which would have been quite an adventure! But then he allowed us to continue and normality was sadly returned to, including my earache and those rotten thoughts. (I don't blame that policeman for stopping us. He was only doing his job.)

The love feast this evening cheered me up a bit, and, to my surprise, 'Socks' was a great success. Peter came along as well, and joined us in a few of the games. Then, before leaving, he handed me a letter from my parents in which they fully forgave me for my past behaviour, and actually asked *me* for forgiveness for the way they'd sometimes treated me. Peter forgave me as well, which was nice.

But I still have that terrible earache. I hope it doesn't stop me from getting to sleep.

16th August (Thursday):

Well, I didn't get much sleep last night. My earache is worse and so are my thoughts. Now I feel like God doesn't love me any more. For once, I decided to have a quiet time on this outreach, but there were so many distractions that I just couldn't concentrate. All the other men in the hall were either making paper aeroplanes out of the tracts or walking on their hands in their sleeping bags. It was hard concentrating on God in Lambeth Baths as well. The person in the shower cubicle next to mine insisted on singing a Beatles medly for half an hour.

I told a few of the leaders about my earache this evening, so they gathered round me in the coffee bar and prayed for me. It was kind of them to do this, but unfortunately nothing happened and my earache is still here. I'm not going to let this get me down, though. God still loves me, and I love God—and I'm determined to get a good night's sleep.

17th August (Friday):

Praise God! My earache's gone! I had a great night's sleep, and when I woke up it had disappeared!

It was our last day of street work today, which was

sad, but also exciting since a number of people gave their lives to the Lord, including some of the children at the children's club. All this in spite of the fact that the last performance of 'Hands' was nearly ruined by a member of our team shouting out 'Socks!' just before the opening line. Luckily I managed to restrain my laughter, but I didn't restrain my cautionary words with him afterwards.

I've been saving all my crisp packets during this outreach, and now I have more than enough to send off for my free 'Indiana Jones and the Temple of Doom' posters. I was tempted to write my name down on the order form as 'Andrew Wooding: The Temple of the Holy Spirit'.

18th August (Saturday):

As well as cleaning up the base today, there were also quite a few water fights—and much of the water was directed at me and a couple of friends. Someone hid everyone's sleeping bags in the spare room last night, and just because we were first back from the coffee bar, people assumed it was us. (Actually they were right, but we didn't let on!) I pity one of the leaders. At one point during the clean-up session, about twenty of the men pinned him down while a bucket of cold water was emptied onto his head. All good clean fun!

To officially end the outreach, all three London teams met at a church in Kennington this evening for a worship service. Some of the new converts came along as well, and so did those punk rockers. It was a fitting end to the most enjoyable three weeks of my life. When I looked around during that service, and saw the radiant faces of my colleagues, I felt so privileged to be a part of this whole thing, and was overwhelmed with awe for the God I'm only just beginning to know.

We're now back in the boys' tent at Holmsted, and I desperately want to leave. We'll be dismissed from this DTS on Wednesday, but until then we have to hang around here to collect our DTS certificates and to sit through another couple of lectures. I've never been too good at goodbyes, and I want to get this over and done with as soon as possible.

19th August (Sunday):

There was a torch fight in the tent last night: people shining their torches in each other's faces and making hand shadows of Bible characters on the roof of the tent. It's quieter than animal noises, but just as disruptive, and, consequently, I didn't get much sleep.

After church this morning most people either snoozed or packed their cases ready to leave Holmsted. I did both, much to the shock of the lady in charge of the attic. You see, she promised to meet me by the attic door at 2 pm to let me in to get my suitcase. She was late, however, and since I felt shattered I lay down in the wash area next to the attic for a quick snooze. But I was soon awoken by a piercing scream. The lady had seen me flat out on the floor and assumed I was dead or had had a heart attack or something. She nearly killed me when I assured her I was still alive. People can be funny sometimes.

I also did some laundry today, and my sleeping bag was the first thing to go in the machine. It doesn't belong to me, you see, and I wanted to get the squashed banana stain out before returning it to its owners. At the washing line I was reunited with my socks, and I was so happy that I nearly kissed them. I have a changed heart. I'm no longer going to take my socks for granted, and I now see them in a new light.

Speaking of seeing things in a new light, I hope there's not another torch fight tonight.

20th August (Monday):

There was a lecture in the barn this morning, although for the life of me I can't remember what it was about. All I remember is nodding off just after praise and worship, then someone prodding me when it was time to leave. There were more fun and games with torches last night so I needed to catch up on my sleep.

A relaxing day really. I did more packing, played some volley-ball, and had an interesting conversation with an American friend about all the exciting possibilities for *Star Trek IV*.

Even though I ate masses of junk food on the outreach, I actually lost a lot of weight. It must have been all the walking around we did and the nervous energy of working on the streets. Also, I wasn't chosen to give my testimony on the outreach, which was a definite answer to prayer.

God is good to me, even though my colleagues aren't. They're now making shadows of animals on the roof of the tent, and also providing the sound effects. It's our last night together tomorrow, thank goodness.

21st August (Tuesday):

We had our last small group period in the barn today, and it was so much fun. Another small group tried to

83

meet at the other end of the barn, but soon had to find a more suitable meeting place because we were laughing too loud and disrupting their prayer time. Many gifts and farewell cards were exchanged during this period, and masses of Swiss chocolate was consumed as well.

Then we had our final meeting together as a DTS. First there was praise and worship, then speeches by a few of the leaders, and then each of the three small teams gathered at the centre of the room to be prayed for. After these prayers, we were each handed a posh certificate to prove that we've successfully completed a Discipleship Training School.

I still don't have a moustache, I'm afraid—just a few bristles. If there's no decent growth by the time we leave for Denmark, I'm going to shave it all off.

22nd August (Wednesday):

None of us could get to sleep last night, but for once I actually didn't mind. This was the last time most of us were probably going to see each other again (until heaven, of course), so we made the most of it by staying up all night, chatting and joking.

It was a very sad day, but I think I handled it maturely. People kept leaving at different times throughout the morning, and there were lots of emotional farewells.

I was one of the last to leave. After another haircut from Laurie (who's finally given up on bringing my hair into the twentieth century), I was driven up to Birmingham where I'm staying with my aunt and uncle. Holmsted's accountant and a fellow student had to drive to Birmingham themselves, so they kindly allowed me to join them. For most of the journey I pretended to be asleep in the back of the car while listening to them talking about all the fun times we've had, and how sad it is that it's now all over.

Yes, it's pretty sad really. But there's also the six weeks in Denmark, isn't there! That should be fun as well. I think....

Copenhagen

1st September (Saturday):

Holmsted Manor is quiet at the moment. I came back this morning, and was surprised to find that the only people here are the house staff, a few of the leaders, the Denmark team (of course) and some of the Northern Ireland team who will be leaving on Monday. I keep expecting to bump into old friends every time I turn round a corner, but most of them aren't here any more. Very disconcerting.

The Denmark team had a meeting tonight in Ellinor Stig's room. Her husband, Per Eivind, is in Denmark at the moment, making arrangements for the YWAM base that they're planning to start there next year. It was a fun meeting really—very informal. I still don't know much about what we'll be doing over the next six weeks, but that's okay. It's probably best for me to remain ignorant of all the possible hardships while there's still a chance for me to run away!

2nd September (Sunday):

Nothing much happened today, which was fine by me since it gave me a chance to get to know some of my fellow team members a bit better, mostly over volleyball or in the Denmark team meeting. There are twelve people on our team altogether, including one couple. Their ages range from twenty (which is me) to about thirty-two, and the nations represented include England, America, Switzerland, Australia and South Africa.

One member of the team somehow managed to grow a thick moustache during our short break. I don't know how he did it, and I'm ever so jealous. I've finally shaved off *my* excuse for a 'moustache'. I'm disappointed, naturally, but I'm trying to look on the positive side. At least I won't have to shave now for a couple of weeks.

3rd September (Monday):

Holmsted Manor is noisy again. The new DTS arrived today, and I was allowed to sit in on their introductory session in the dining room. I secretly took my diary in with me, and laughed as I read about *my* first day here. I wonder if any of the new people are as petrified as I was?

Keith read the team a letter today, telling us what we'll be doing in Denmark. It was from Ida, a doctor in Copenhagen who's single-handedly organized our outreach, basically by looking up local churches in the telephone book and calling the pastors to see if they want our help.

None of the things she told us sounded too bad,

except for one request she made at the end of her letter. She's going to be testing a new antibiotic soon, and wondered if a few of us would give blood samples before and after taking it! Not surprisingly, there was a massed hush when this was announced—and I think most of us got the *point*! (Just trying to *inject* a little humour there).

I hope our journey goes smoothly tomorrow.

4th September (Tuesday):

Picture this if you will: twelve sweaty youths with tons of luggage trying to travel on the London Underground during the morning rush hour; twelve tired and sweaty youths dragging their luggage on and off trains and the ferry all day long; and twelve annoyed, tired and sweaty youths trying to get to sleep in two cramped cabins of the train from Holland to Denmark, with customs guards waking us up every hour or so to see our passports.

That's all I'm going to write about our journey so far. I want to forget today as soon as possible, and keeping an in-depth account of my day-long sulking fit is not going to help. Besides, it's hard to write while travelling over seventy miles an hour.

5th September (Wednesday):

We made it! Jan, our translator for the first half of the outreach, met us all at Copenhagen train station at 7 am and drove us over to the Pentecostal church where we'll be staying for the next three weeks.

After tucking into breakfast with the pastor and his family (strong coffee and open-faced cheese sandwiches), our team went for a walk along the Copenhagen walking street. Copenhagen is alive with people right now—especially since this is the middle of the tourist season—but spiritually it seems dead. I'm not going to jump to premature conclusions, though. I remember being pessimistic about England, and was pleasantly surprised with the success of our three weeks in London. Maybe we'll be successful here as well.

When we got back, we tidied up and put our sleeping bags in place. (The boys and girls will be sleeping in separate rooms next to the ground floor hall.) Then Keith split us up into two intercession groups that will meet together every morning, and Laurie wrote up a work duty rota for us. *My* work duty is to clean the toilets, worst luck.

We had more bread and cheese for lunch. The cheese smells awful, but tastes absolutely wonderful. I think I'm going to like it here.

6th September (Thursday):

A number of the team had nightmares last night, including me. I dreamt that I was witnessing to some punk rockers outside an Egyptian temple. They weren't very interested in what I said, so when we parted company, I walked up the steps to the temple and started praying for them. Then, instead of feeling the peace of the Holy Spirit, I was overwhelmed by what I can only describe as the most evil presence I have ever felt. I could put the dream down to all the cheese I've been having, but I'm pretty sure it's Satan trying to discourage me.

We did our first work as a team today. The boys

helped clean the windows of the church, while the girls delivered tracts through letter boxes. And Jan started building a kitchen next to the ground floor hall. Unfortunately, we have to clean windows again tomorrow. I can't wait to do some *real* work. Now that I'm more spiritual, I want the Lord to use me in miracles and signs and wonders and all that kind of thing.

7th September (Friday):

I had another bad dream last night. It wasn't exactly a nightmare, but it was still pretty rotten. I dreamt I was visiting Holmsted Manor and no one could remember me, and, consequently, I felt intense rejection when I woke up. Other team members had rotten dreams as well, so after breakfast and quiet time we split up into our two intercession groups and prayed for the Lord to protect us while we sleep so that we won't have these sorts of dreams again. Then we met together again to practise some songs and to talk about all the dramas we're going to be rehearsing.

Per Eivind Stig dropped by for a few moments this afternoon, to encourage us in our work so far (cleaning windows, big deal), and to give us a progress report on YWAM, Denmark. We won't be seeing him for a while now since he's going back to England, which is a shame. His presence cheered us up a lot, and it also gave me an excuse not to clean windows for a while.

We all walked over to Ida's house this evening to thank her for the work she's done for us. Ida was great, and she treated us all to coffee and pastries—but we deliberately kept quiet about that blood business she mentioned in her letter. She lives on the grounds of a hospital, and most of her instruments of torture are on display in the house.

8th September (Saturday):

No nightmares last night—just a general lack of sleep among our team. Keith reckoned it was because we've been drinking too much of this strong Danish coffee, and I think he's right. We vowed at our team meeting to try and cut down from now on.

Work duty was fun today. I was sent out to buy a screwdriver, so I 'accidentally-on-purpose' got lost and arrived back at the church just after all the windows had been cleaned. What a pleasant surprise!

In the evening we were invited over to the house of the pastor of a big Lutheran church. After a hearty meal (followed by two generous servings of ice-cream!), she asked to hear one of our songs. We complied with an impromptu rendition of 'Shout for Joy', and since the second verse was 'Jump for Joy' we enthusiastically jumped up and down in time with the beat. This was a terrible mistake. Her house was filled with antiques, and as we jumped they dangerously bounced along her shelves. There was also an old lady living downstairs, we were informed afterwards, who probably didn't appreciate all our thumping. Still, our host was very good about the whole thing and she complimented us on our singing.

I only had six cups of coffee today which is a definite improvement. I also had three Danish pastries. Those things are addictive.

9th September (Sunday):

We performed some songs at the Pentecostal church service this morning, and then Laurie gave the sermon (which was translated by Jan). The congregation here are very friendly, and surprisingly most of them speak English. (Apparently everyone in Denmark has to learn English at school, which means we shouldn't have many language problems when we work on the streets.) Afterwards, I read a few comics that I had brought from England, and wrote a few letters. A very relaxing day.

That team member absent-mindedly shaved off his moustache this morning, which gave me a good laugh. But then he told me he wasn't too upset since he'll probably grow it back again in a couple of weeks. The rotter!

10th September (Monday):

I was a bit frustrated today since it was our first day off and I didn't have any money to spend. Good old Laurie came to my rescue in the evening though by loaning me the money to go to Tivoli gardens with some of the rest of the team. Tivoli looks amazing— especially at night when all the lights are on—but afterwards we went to a free classical music concert that was ultra-boring. Still it was fun being with other team members, and I got a lot of letter writing done during the Mozart symphony.

Any day now I should receive a letter from my parents with more of my savings. It had better come soon. I'm rapidly running out of clean clothes, and I'm scared that I won't have any money for the launderette. I definitely don't want a repeat of the sock episode.

11th September (Tuesday):

We're going to be working with a Lutheran church for the next five days, helping them with street evangelism. Sounds exciting, doesn't it! Not really. For two whole hours today my partner and I walked up and down a busy Copenhagen street trying to witness to people. Our results? Not a sausage. No one wanted to talk to us, and everyone seemed to be in a rush. Often we'd say hello to someone, and they'd walk straight past us as if we weren't there.

Later, we met with some members of the church. We one-by-one introduced ourselves (with Jan translating, of course), taught them three English praise songs, and then Keith spoke for a while about evangelism. In return we were offered more strong coffee and pastries which I was much too polite to refuse.

Keith cycled over to Ida's post box when we got back, but there was nothing for me from my parents...or from anyone else I know for that matter. It's hard having nothing to read while everyone else is engrossed in their post and passing on new bits of gossip. Jan tried to cheer me up by showing me how to make a silly noise with my hands, but it didn't work. Hopefully I'll get some post tomorrow.

12th September (Wednesday):

We did more work on that street today, and we were just as unsuccessful, if not more so. Keith told us that if we got bored we could browse inside the shops for a while—something that most of us took advantage of. This was also frustrating, though, because I still don't have any money to buy anything.

There was no post for me again this evening, although nearly everyone else got something. I tried to impress people with that new hand trick that Jan taught me last night, but most were too busy reading news from friends or relatives.

Instead I listened to the BBC World Service on my radio, and got steadily more homesick for England. This outreach isn't turning out at all like I imagined. I want to go home.

13th September (Thursday):

More work on the streets today, this time with some volunteers from the church. Then in the evening we attended a nearby house fellowship, introducing ourselves, singing a few songs, and listening to the teaching by the house fellowship leader (which was quietly translated for us by Jan).

A Danish girl came up to me afterwards and asked me some questions about England. I soon realized that she wasn't a Christian, so I promptly steered the conversation to more spiritual matters. I told her in detail what God means to me, and she seemed engrossed, listening intently to every word. We spoke for over an hour, although it didn't seem like it. And Laurie told me afterwards that I ate three pastries during the course of the conversation, which I honestly don't remember! I'd better keep praying for this girl.

Nothing from my parents yet, although I did get a postcard of a monkey eating a banana. It doesn't really count though since it was sent by one of the team members who'd taken pity on me.

None of our team have had bad dreams these last few nights, so God has answered our prayers!

14th September (Friday):

I wish everyone in Denmark was as open as that girl last night. We were witnessing with volunteers from the Lutheran church again today, and *no one* wanted to stop and talk! In the end I gave up trying to speak to people and just handed out loads of Danish tracts.

We had more coffee and pastries when we got back to the church, and then we were invited to an afternoon service. It's our last day with this church tomorrow. We'll be doing two open airs with them (which I'm quite excited about), and we'll also be premiering some of the dramas we've been rehearsing every morning (which I'm *not* excited about). Maybe the Danes will be more receptive to the gospel after an open air...or maybe not. We'll have to wait and see.

I got another Danish postcard today, this time of a monkey smoking a cigar. Obviously that team member took pity on my abysmal lack of post again.

15th September (Saturday):

I don't remember 'The Chicken Sketch' ever being so poorly received. There we were on that street again, loudly clucking like chickens and enthusiastically diving in and out of people like out-of-control aeroplanes, and everyone just walked straight past us as if we weren't there. One of our team members got a bit frustrated when he gave his testimony, so he shouted as loud as he could into the microphone to try and get people to listen. This got us into a bit of trouble since a funeral was being held at the church across the street and someone had to come and tell us to quieten down a bit. In spite of all this, the volunteers were great. One of them even prayed for someone's sore leg to be healed—and it was!

Great! My money came today, and a letter from my parents. Now I can go to the launderette.

16th September (Sunday):

One of the elders at the Pentecostal church drove me and two other team members over to a castle this afternoon and I pretended to be interested. The castle was full of paintings of historical Danish battles, all of them bloody and all of them apparently in the name of Christianity.

I was quite depressed when we got back, so I went for a walk with *War* by U2 on my Walkman and understood for the first time the words to 'Drowning Man'. It seemed as if God was singing them to me, telling me to take his hand and to hold on tightly to his love, because the storm would soon pass. I feel in danger of drowning on this outreach (metaphorically, of course), and I have a choice. Either I allow myself to slip into apathy and self-pity, or I hold on tightly to him so that he can lift me up and strengthen me.

The choice isn't as easy as it seems, and apathy is already creeping in.

17th September (Monday):

It was stupid of me to get depressed yesterday. We had another day off today, and I thoroughly enjoyed myself.

The day got off to a particularly good start at the breakfast table which, in stark contrast to breakfasts at Holmsted Manor, is always lively. An English chap on our team did an excellent Worzel Gommidge impression, Jan made more silly noises with his hands, and I told everyone how I once tried to become a black-and-white minstrel by covering my face with shoe polish.

In the afternoon, I went for a walk round town with a couple of team members. We went to see the Little Mermaid statue (which was smaller than I expected), then walked through a park on the way back and discovered to our delight that the conker season is now upon us. We had a competition to see who could collect the most conkers before getting back, and I won!

It's fun being a kid again! I recommend it to everyone. What a great day! (But I didn't get any more post.)

18th September (Tuesday):

We had to teach at a confirmation class this morning at a nearby Lutheran church. Quite enjoyable I suppose, although it's hard pretending to be the most joyful Christian ever to a bunch of uninterested kids at 8 am. We have to teach another class tomorrow, which means waking up early again. Groan.

When we got back I offered to fetch the mail from Ida's post box. I enjoyed the forty-minute walk there, eagerly anticipating the many letters I would receive from my buddies around the world, then spent the forty minutes back fuming at my fellow team members because they received post and I didn't.

My bad mood disappeared by dinner time so I told everyone how I once tried to poison my mum. When I was alone in the house I mixed all sorts of substances in a bowl (Jif lemon juice, chocolate ice-cream, HP Sauce, etc.), but when she got back she refused to eat this unappetizing mixture. So she's still alive today.

Laurie changed the work duty rota today, but she didn't appoint me as one of the cooks. I wonder why?

19th September (Wednesday):

Another confirmation class this morning, and then in the afternoon we had drama practice and free time. I wasted *my* free time by walking to the post box again and getting absolutely nothing. Before the end of this outreach I want at least one letter from someone who's not a relative or a pitying team member.

This evening we went out walking with members of the Pentecostal church to hand out tracts and hopefully bring non-Christians back to the church to witness to them. We didn't have much success I'm afraid, and the only people who came back to the church with us were two drunks with guitars who insisted on singing us old rock and roll numbers all evening. I was tempted to sing along with them, but thought it might be a bad example. So I contented myself with devouring most of the Danish butter cookies on the table while imagining all the possible letters that are on their way to me. Maybe I'll get one tomorrow.

20th September (Thursday):

Keith and Laurie arranged for us to work at a coffee bar this evening in Copenhagen's red light district, run by a team from a nearby charismatic church. I wasn't too enthusiastic about this at first, but once we hit the streets my attitude rapidly changed.

The first person my partner and I talked to was a backslidden Christian who admitted that he probably wasn't living the way God wants him to. That was obvious since he was engrossed in a pornographic window display when we approached him. We must have talked for over half-an-hour, and he asked us why, out of everyone in the red light district, we chose to speak to him. I think he suspected that God was chasing him, and he was probably right! Two other team members soon joined us, and we prayed for him right there on the street. When we'd finished we saw that there were tears in his eyes, but before we could say anything he quickly said goodbye and walked away. The Lord was obviously convicting him very strongly!

There were conversations like that all evening. Isn't it funny that the people who seem most sinful are more aware of their need for God! I can't wait to work here again.

21st September (Friday):

Well, it's been a pretty routine day really: intercession, drama, and more bread and smelly cheese for lunch. A new type of cheese turned up at the dinner table today. It's called Norwegian goat cheese, and it tastes a lot like fudge. Keith and I seem to be the only people on the team who like it, which is good because it means there's all the more for us!

At 6 pm our team parted ways. A camp is being held for the youth of the Pentecostal church this weekend, and Laurie and most of our team travelled with them. Keith and three others (including me) stayed behind, and we're going to be joining them there tomorrow morning.

The reason we stayed behind was to attend the youth group meeting of another Lutheran church in Copenhagen. (There's a lot of them here!) We didn't actually say much at the meeting—just briefly introduced ourselves and sang a few songs—but it was certainly a relaxing evening and I'm glad we went.

I'm looking forward to our trip tomorrow. Despite my love of cities, I'm getting bored with Copenhagen and I want to see more of Denmark.

22nd September (Saturday):

I haven't a clue which part of Denmark we're in, but wherever we are it's incredible! The four of us arrived just in time to hear the first lecture this morning which I'm sure was good, but the person who translated for us had to whisper and I didn't hear a word. So I just stared out of the window, dying to explore the Danish countryside.

Which is exactly what I did when the lecture had finished. Quite spectacular, although it's not as nice as the English countryside. (But don't take my word for it. I'm biased in case you hadn't already guessed!) I had my quiet time on a nearby beach, which was spooky because I was alone there and it seemed like I was the only person left on earth. Yet I felt incredibly close to God while praying.

This evening was even more incredible. After another lecture, most of us went for a walk along the beach in the darkness. Wow. Because we're away from any big cities, the sky was totally clear and was full of stars: stars above us, stars behind us, and stars straight ahead just above the horizon. And the sand on the beach was phosphorescent which meant that when you scraped it it shone in the dark.

It's a shame we're leaving already tomorrow. I'm enjoying it here.

23rd September (Sunday):

Yes, well as much as I like the youth from this church I'm glad they're not with us again tonight. I didn't get much sleep last night, basically because some of the more rowdy youth in our dorm decided to have a late-night shaving cream fight, and I was one of the victims. And someone with an air pistol thought it would be 'absolutely hilarious' if he quietly opened the door to the girls' dorm and shot a blank at the ceiling. It certainly woke a number of people up (actually, it woke *everyone* up), but I don't think many of them found it funny.

Most of the youth here are super, however, especially the ones I peeled the potatoes with this morning. They have a great sense of humour, and I even joined in a water fight with them. (I suppose that's just as bad as a shaving cream fight, isn't it! I can joke around with the best of them until I want to get to sleep, and then I always qualify for the 'grouch of the world' award.)

We arrived back in Copenhagen just in time for the evening service at the Pentecostal church, where a number of the youth group told the congregation what the Lord had done for them this weekend. I didn't understand a word they were saying, but I could tell they'd been blessed.

And so had I. I'm never going to forget those stars last night.

24th September (Monday):

I don't think I've ever been so scared in my entire life. A team member and I decided to explore a community in Copenhagen today called 'Christiania'. A big mistake. Christiania is almost as big as Disneyland, but it's definitely not for kids. It's inhabited entirely by drug addicts, hell's angels, devil worshippers, and, worst of all, hundreds of ginormous dogs. (I've been petrified of dogs ever since I was attacked by one at school.)

At one point in our travels, we had to pass a pack of particularly ferocious-looking dogs. 'Don't worry,' my friend assured me. 'Just act calm and they won't bother you.' So we quickly walked past with me quietly praying all the time, and, breathing a sigh of relief, I looked back just in time to see one of the dogs go for an old lady. The lady yelled, and so did I.

Eventually, after an interminable two hours in that place, we made our way back out and each took a photo of the entrance. Just then, an overweight hippy waddled up to us and loudly warned, 'If you take any photos inside, you're dead!' And he effectively illustrated this by dragging his index finger across his throat. We both gulped and headed quickly back to the Pentecostal church.

I'm still shaking.

25th September (Tuesday):

On Thursday evening there's going to be a healing service at a Lutheran church just up the road. Our team has been invited to take part, and, starting today, we had to knock on people's doors and hand them leaflets announcing the service (and hopefully witness to them as well). I didn't witness to many people today, and I think my partner got a bit fed up with me. Every time we rang a doorbell and a dog started barking, I would immediately run away and let *her* do all the talking. Everyone here seems to have large aggressive dogs!

We have to do this again tomorrow. Groan.

26th September (Wednesday):

After delivering leaflets again and meeting more rotten dogs, a few members of the Pentecostal church joined us this evening for an open air. I dread to think what they must think of us. *They* did marvellously, expertly singing Danish praise songs and giving testimonies. But about the only thing *we* contributed, apart from a testimony in English, was a drama called 'Man Can' which went fine until one of the actors shouted one of his lines just a bit too loud. Then we all got the giggles and couldn't stop laughing while trying to say our lines. What made it worse for me was that two of our more lively spectators kept running in and out of us, sniffing our shoes and barking unsettlingly loudly. (They were dogs, in case you hadn't guessed.)

I was too tired to walk to Ida's post box today so I let Keith cycle there, and I'm glad I did. Not a sausage for me again, as usual. I miss England terribly.

27th September (Thursday):

I must admit that I had some doubts today about that Lutheran church. A strange choir was practising some spooky music there this morning, which unsettled me a bit. And when our team arrived there for the healing service we all felt like we'd just walked out of a time machine. The inside of the church is very old-fashioned, and the pastor wore what looked like a sixteenth-century robe.

It wasn't long, however, before my reservations disappeared. I had to give my testimony this evening, and instead of speaking to a load of tired, uninterested people (which is what I'd expected), most of the congregation positively beamed at me, delighted with what the Lord had done in my life. And when the pastor prayed for people during the time of healing it was almost like looking into the face of Jesus. His smile was so radiant.

I wonder if *my* face ever reminds people of Jesus? To be honest, I don't think most of the time it does.

28th September (Friday):

Well, our three weeks with the Pentecostal church are now over, and since we don't have anywhere to stay in Cophenhagen till Sunday, we travelled to Randers (Jan's home town) today for a well-earned break. The guys will be sleeping on the floor of Jan's parents' house while we're here, and the girls will be sleeping in Lisbeth's house, our translator for the second half of the outreach.

I'm going to be doing a lot of praying while in Randers. We've only been in Denmark about three-

and-a-half weeks, and already it seems like we've been here for ever. I've also lost a lot of my joy.

Hopefully these new surroundings will help me forget about my homesickness for England for a while.

29th September (Saturday):

During a walk round Randers this morning, I realized that I haven't been spending much time with the Lord since we arrived in Denmark. Maybe that's why my joy has gone and I've been feeling so homesick. Come on, Andrew. Just because you're on a YWAM outreach team, it doesn't automatically elevate you to the status of super-Christian. It's your prayer relationship with the Lord that counts. Shape up! (It's hard to summon up enough energy to shape up, though, when you don't have much joy.)

There was a surprise party for the New Zealander on our team this evening, with a slap-up meal cooked by Jan's parents and then some party games. Great fun.

Not fun enough to get my mind off England, though. I'm definitely going to have to start praying more.

30th September (Sunday):

Christianity. What's it all about?

All the way back to Copenhagan I tried to figure out what makes someone a good Christian. Faithfully reading the Bible every day? Not necessarily. Listening to loads of Christian teaching tapes? No. Anyone can listen to tapes. Getting involved with a small weekly Bible study and having lots of deep theological discussions? Doing a DTS?

I've been deceiving myself. All of the above are fine, but having Christian friends and getting involved in Christian activities doesn't mean that my relationship with the Lord leaves nothing to be desired. Have I *really* made him the Lord of my life, or am I still living for myself, only occasionally turning to him for help?

I've decided to humble myself before the Lord more once we're back in England and I feel better about everything. Before then, to make things easy, I'm just going to lie back, relax, and enjoy the rest of the outreach by not taking things too seriously. I hope God doesn't mind.

We're staying in an apostolic church this week, having open airs on the walking street every day and handing out leaflets advertising their five-day evangelistic rally that starts tomorrow. I hope we have more success with our open airs than before.

1st October (Monday):

I felt guilty during intercession this morning, and wasn't sure why. I thought it might be the devil giving me condemnation to reduce my effectiveness as an evangelist, but no matter how much I rebuked it, the guilt just wouldn't go away. The open airs weren't much fun either. It rained nearly the whole time we were outside, and our second open air drew the phenomenal 'crowd' of two old ladies and a poodle.

The first evangelistic meeting was held in the church hall tonight, and quite a few people became Christians. Absolutely wonderful, of course, but I must admit that my mind was elsewhere.

Afterwards, most of our team raided the kitchen for late-night snacks. In an attempt to liven up my day, I poured a substantial amount of pepper on my hankie and sniffed it up my left nostril to see what would happen. 'Atchsplerge!' was my next reaction (*and* the reaction after that, and so on and so on), and before long I was the only person left in the kitchen.

Sniffing that pepper was probably the single most stupid thing I have ever done in my entire life (aside from covering my face with shoe polish, that is). Never mind. God still loves me. Or does he?

2nd October (Tuesday):

Well, it looks like the Denmark team still loves me at least. Instead of intercession this morning, we all sat round a table and handed notes of encouragement to each other. Here are some of the comments *I* received:

'Your sense of humour is a real blessing to me.'

'I like your sense of humour.'

'Your sense of humour is something I'll never forget in the whole world.'

And: 'You are a beautiful person, and I love you dearly.' (This last comment was written by me!)

There was another evangelistic meeting tonight with more people giving their lives to the Lord. And then there was another meeting of the Denmark team around the fridge.

Someone on the team doesn't appreciate my sense of humour *that* much. The pepper pot has been hidden!

3rd October (Wednesday):

The evangelistic meeting was held in a local theatre this evening, and the message was given by some American preacher with whom I wasn't too impressed.

What he said certainly sounded very appealing, but there was nothing about repentance from sins and the cost of discipleship. He made God sound like Father Christmas, a lovable old man who gives out loads of toys and sweets but doesn't require anything on our part.

After the preacher had given the altar call, he told all the new converts to go back into the audience. None of them had filled out cards with their names and addresses, and he obviously didn't see the need for follow-up work. Then he started ranting on about healing, and kept telling people off for their lack of faith when they weren't healed.

I'm surprised there isn't smoke coming out of my nose, not because of the pepper but because of how angry I am. Unfortunately, this preacher is going to be speaking at the theatre for the next two nights.

4th October (Thursday):

I had to wash up with another team member after lunch today, and just for a laugh we washed two of the disposable paper plates we'd eaten off and hung them on the outdoor washing line. I wonder how long it'll take other team members to notice!

Keith said I didn't have to go to the evangelistic meeting this evening, so I prayed while walking round town instead. Then I telephoned my parents in California to tell them how much I miss them, and, more importantly, to have them send some more of my savings since I've just about run out of money again. I could believe for God to provide the money himself, I suppose, but I don't have that much faith.

5th October (Friday):

Laurie told me off today for criticizing that preacher so much. She agreed with me that his presentation left much to be desired, but I have no right to question his commitment to the Lord. Only God can do that. She was right, of course, and I was prepared to forgive him for everything when I saw the fruits of his ministry first-hand at this evening's meeting.

The theatre was packed since it was the final evening of the rally, and three people turned up from that Lutheran church that we worked with the second week we were here. We knew they weren't saved, so while the preacher gave his message we kept praying for them to give their lives to the Lord. Sure enough, they practically ran to the front during the altar call and some of us went with them to encourage them.

The atmosphere up front was electric, and we could sense the power of God very strongly. All three were gloriously saved, and all three had tears in their eyes when we left the theatre. It's moments like these that make this whole outreach worth while. Praise the Lord!

(I was also pleased to see that they'd given their names and addresses to the church counsellors. Obviously some of the pastors have had firm words with the preacher about follow-up arrangements.)

6th October (Saturday):

We didn't really have to, but Keith and Laurie insisted we do one last open air for the apostolic church. I'm glad they did.

At first it looked as though it was going to be a

disaster. Just before starting, representatives of the Danish humanist party parked themselves across the street from us to shout various humanistic things at people, and a few seconds into praise and worship the rain began pouring down.

Most of us felt like going back to the church and calling it a day, but Laurie insisted that we pray for the weather to change. So we split up into small intercession groups, and not much later (to my astonished surprise!) the clouds parted and the sun shone down. Then, after moving up the street away from the humanists, we had our best open air so far on this outreach. A group of local Christians joined us in praise and worship. (They were just about to perform their own open air and had seen us.) People actually stopped to watch our dramas for a change, and a group of us had a really good conversation with an English tourist who'd been thinking a lot recently about the meaning of life. It was refreshing to talk to someone who was actually interested in what we had to say. When I looked up at the sky I could almost see God looking down at us and saying, 'Well done. I'm pleased with you all.'

Even though a lot of people did laundry today, no one has noticed those paper plates yet on the washing line. My co-conspirator and I are very disappointed.

7th October (Sunday):

Originally we were going to leave the apostolic church today, but because we don't have anywhere to sleep next week, we've been allowed to stay a bit longer. The congregation here are wonderful. After the service this morning, many of them handed us bag-loads of food to show their appreciation for the work we've done for their church. One of the bags contained about twenty servings of liver. Yum.

Before dinner I took those plates down from the washing line, then asked everyone at the dinner table if they'd noticed them. No one answered. They were all too busy making funny faces and groaning at their liver. I don't know why they seemed so miserable. *My* liver was great, and I even had seconds. Lisbeth tried to lighten the atmosphere by telling a joke about marmalade, but it didn't seem to work. Honestly, some people are such fuss-pots!

It's our first free day tomorrow since we got back from Randers. I think I'll have a lie-in.

8th October (Monday):

So much for my lie-in. I woke up at 6 am, and no matter how hard I tried I just couldn't get back to sleep. All the while I kept thinking that maybe I should be praying, but I just didn't have the energy.

Eventually I made it to the breakfast table for my morning ration of cornflakes, and then I walked to Ida's post box. Nothing for me as usual I'm afraid, but when I got back Keith read me a letter he'd received from Per Eivind. Apparently, Per Eivind needs volunteers for a mobile team he'll be starting next year. The team will be based in Randers, and it'll travel to different Danish churches to preach and perform dramas, and to spread the word about YWAM Denmark. While Keith was reading, I felt that maybe *I* should volunteer for this. 'No, Lord,' I initially protested. 'I'm not coming back to Denmark again. I want to work in England.' But the feeling persisted, so

I wrote a short letter to Per Eivind, asking if he'd be interested in me working on the team.

Isn't it funny. I can't wait to leave Denmark, and yet here I am fully prepared to return. Don't get me wrong. I do *like* Denmark...honestly. It's just that my heart's not fully here at the moment. Maybe it'll be easier for me next year.

Great! Only another ten days until the outreach has finished and we can all go home!

9th October (Tuesday):

The Lord can use anything, I suppose, and that includes my fear of dogs! We had to work in the red light district again this evening, and to get us in the mood for witnessing, Laurie (my partner) and I walked up and down a dark side-street for a while, praying out loud.

It was down that street that we encountered a prostitute called Anna. (Her name has been changed—not to protect her but because I can't remember it.) For some reason, Anna didn't like us praying on her territory and she promptly shouted lots of rude things at us. I know you might say, 'Sticks and stones may break my bones, etc.,' but her small (but extremely loud) dachshund felt the same way about us. Luckily it was on a lead, but I still hid in the shadows, afraid that its owner would let it loose at any moment to eat me alive.

Ignoring the barrage of insults (and barks), Laurie started a conversation with Anna and discovered that she'd become a prostitute to support her heroin habit. Laurie told Anna about Jesus and how he could release her from that habit, and then looked impatiently at me. 'Come on, Andrew!' she shouted. 'I'm telling her that the Lord can set her free from heroin, and you're scared of a stupid dog!' And before I could say anything in defence, Laurie pointed a finger at me and commanded: 'In the name of Jesus, I rebuke that fear of dogs in you!'

It's lucky I'm a good actor. I honestly don't think I was healed of doggiephobia, but I realized then that if I continued avoiding her dachshund, Anna would doubt the healing power of God. So, gulping, I boldly stepped towards them all to prove that I'd been 'healed'. Anna seemed impressed, but her rotten dog obviously wasn't since it kept on barking at me.

Eventually we made it back to the coffee bar. Anna made a real commitment to the Lord this evening, and was completely delivered from her addiction to heroin. She looked so peaceful after we'd prayed with her, but her dog seemed just as unhappy as ever.

Praise God for Anna's new life in the Lord!

Nine days until we leave Denmark....

10th October (Wednesday):

Now I've even grown weary of the red light district. I felt like I was just going through the motions when we worked there this evening, and all the challenge and the excitement had gone. I love Lisbeth. I love Jan. I love our team. And I love *everyone* we've worked with in Denmark so far (well, almost). But...I don't know. I've gone through a DTS, a summer camp, a three-week outreach in London, and almost six weeks in Denmark, and I've been surrounded for the last five months by people, people, people. I guess I'm just tired, and I want to be on my own for a while.

(The real reason I'm fed up with the red light district is that it was wet on the streets this evening, and the holes in my shoes let the water in.)

Maybe I won't feel so self-analytical after I've had a good night's sleep.

Eight days until we leave Denmark....

11th October (Thursday):

Everyone who had fully paid their outreach fees got a refund this afternoon from Keith. Apparently this outreach is turning out cheaper than he and Laurie expected, especially after all the free meals we've been treated to and the food we were given on Sunday. Remember I called my parents last week for more money? Well, it looks like the Lord's blessed me in spite of my lack of faith. Hallelujah!

I don't think the rest of our team are good stewards of their money, though. There were not many people at the dinner table this evening because most of them ate out. I can't think *why* they ate out. There was perfectly good liver for them here, and it was all included in their outreach fees.

Seven more days until we leave....

12th October (Friday):

These dogs in Denmark are vicious, and a lot of them must wait by the door all day for a hand to come through their letter box. We had to deliver tracts today, and I was pushing a tract through *one* letter box when I heard a really loud *snap*! Quickly, I pulled my hand out...and the top half of the tract. The dog was obviously chewing the other half, and I cringed when I realized that could have been some of my fingers.

The streets were wet again today, and I was shivering as my shoes let in more cold water.

'Lord,' I prayed on the way back to the apostolic church, 'I can't carry on like this for much longer. May I have a new pair of shoes, please?' My prayer was soon answered. When we returned, the church's caretaker invited us to take anything we wanted from their spare clothes room. Clothes normally bore me, but there was nothing better for me to do so I joined the rest of the team in there. And while Lisbeth took photos of us all in silly clothes, I found a bright brown pair of shoes that fit me perfectly.

Praise God! The Lord *does* answer prayers! Now I'm praying that Ida will forget she promised to visit us tomorrow to take our blood samples.

Six more days until we leave....

13th October (Saturday):

Despite more near-fatal encounters with dogs, I volunteered to spend an extra couple of hours today delivering tracts (much to the surprise of Keith and Laurie). My act of kindness didn't work, though, because Ida was still at the church when I got back. 'Ah, you're just in time, Andrew,' smiled Ida. 'For a moment there, I thought you wouldn't make it.' And she motioned for me to sit down next to her and her needle. 'Gulp.'

I ate more than usual tonight. Ida's taking more of our blood tomorrow, and I kept kidding myself that I needed extra food to replenish my blood supply.

Five more days....

14th October (Sunday):

Sadly, we had to say goodbye to the apostolic church this afternoon, and we moved back over to the Pentecostal church where we'll be staying until Thursday.

Jan was at the church to greet us when we arrived. He travelled all the way from Randers to spend a couple of days with us before we go back to England. Ida and her needle were also there to greet us.

To replenish my blood supply again this evening, I ate the rest of the liver that was in the fridge, and a couple of apples, and some of those nice home-made biscuits, and that two-week-old banana, and a few other things.

Four more days....

15th October (Monday):

I felt really sick last night, and couldn't get to sleep at all. It must have been all that food I ate.

It was a free day today, so we all went to see a Walt Disney film (which broke down four times), and Jan treated us all to Great Dane ice-cream cones. They tasted wonderful, but were so big that everyone soon felt as nauseous as me.

Jan has to leave again tomorrow. It's sad, but we'll probably meet up again if I work in Randers next year.

On the way back to the church we encountered a peace march. Marching for peace is fine, except a lot of the marchers were dressed in black and had pale white make-up on their faces that made them look as if they were dead. Some were even dressed as witches.

I still feel sick (especially after all that ice-cream). And now I feel a sense of gloom after seeing the people in that march. I should spend some time in the cleansing presence of the Lord, I suppose, but it's late and I need to get some sleep.

Three days....

16th October (Tuesday):

Another rotten night. I didn't get any sleep again, and I was sick a couple of times. It was awful. So was delivering tracts all day, which was even more exhausting than before because we were assigned blocks of flats and had to walk up and down loads of flights of stairs.

Ida treated us all to a farewell meal at her house this evening which was kind of her, although it was hard keeping all the food in. (I still felt nauseous.) Then we had a time of prayer. Ida has not had a good deal of contact with the team these last six weeks, and yet she prayed tonight in great detail for each one of us. I'm always surprised when people remember my name, let alone my future plans, where I come from and how old I am. I was impressed!

Ida's praying made me feel guilty about not spending much time with the Lord recently, so I've decided to fast for the next three days to pray about my future. I won't be able to eat for a while anyway—not with how sick I feel—so fasting is going to be easy.

Two days....

17th October (Wednesday):

I got a lot of exercise today. There was more walking up and down stairs delivering tracts, and then some of us attended a youth group meeting in the evening.

One of the things we had to do at this meeting was play a strenuous running game which was fun at first, but after ten minutes I had to excuse myself to catch my breath, and it took me a whole half-hour to recover. I thought I was going to die!

Okay, so I'm unfit, and maybe I *do* eat the wrong food sometimes. But a person's got to have a few idiosyncrasies like this, hasn't he, otherwise he's boring. (Why do I feel God shaking his head at me while I'm writing this?)

I got that money from my parents today, so now I've got more than enough for my two-week holiday in England before I go back to California. We're leaving for England tomorrow! Fantastic!

18th October (Thursday):

I can't believe it. We're finally on our way home. We tidied up the church today, packed our bags, had one final meal at the Pentecostal church (which I had to abstain from because of my fast), and then we left on the train. Lisbeth, Ida and the three that became Christians at the evangelistic rally were at the station to say goodbye to us.

You know, it was all worth it just for their salvation— *and* for that prostitute in the red light district. I think I had a bad attitude on this outreach. I'll try and do better if Per Eivind accepts me for the mobile team next year.

This fast is doing wonders for my appetite. I couldn't eat two days ago, and now I'm constantly thinking of quarter-pounders with cheese. I haven't prayed much so far, but that's okay. I'll make up for my negligence tomorrow.

19th October (Friday):

Praise God. We're finally back in England—and not a moment too soon. The journey back was just as exhausting as the journey six weeks ago, and my enforced starvation made it seem even longer. I didn't do much praying about my future today—I didn't feel up to it—but I'm sure the Lord's got everything under control.

The house staff at Holmsted held a welcome-back party for us this evening, which was fun, although it was hard saying no to the cream cakes and all the other goodies that were being handed round. Eventually I collected one of everything on a plate, and then at midnight, when my fast was officially over, I devoured the whole lot in one go. I wish I hadn't. It's hard to write when you have chronic indigestion.

I honestly don't know what this fast has accomplished, but at least I can now impress everyone by telling them I didn't eat food for three days.

I officially leave YWAM tomorrow. I wonder what the Lord's got for me next?

12th November (Monday):
(Written in California)

He wants me to join YWAM again, that's what. I got a letter from Ellinor Stig this morning, telling me I've been accepted for the YWAM Denmark mobile team. I start in January, and I'll be there six months.

Am I depressed? Actually, I'm quite excited. It'll be fun travelling round Denmark on this mobile team, and I'll have loads of interesting things to write about. My mind wasn't fully on serving the Lord while I was in Copenhagen, and I certainly didn't do my best to encourage Keith and Laurie or help my fellow team members. But God's given me a second chance, and hopefully my motives are now pure.

Thank you, Lord, for being so patient with me. And thank you also for all the fun things I'll be doing for you next year in Denmark.

I can hardly wait....

The
GO Festival

19th January (Saturday):

Well, here I am. I finally arrived at Randers train station at 8 pm, and was met there by a man whose name I don't remember. We quickly exchanged greetings, and then he drove me to the flat of some people whose names I also don't remember (except for Liv Ella, a Norwegian who was a student on my DTS).

Per Eivind Stig (who lives downstairs) told me when I arrived that there's been a sudden change of plan. A week-long missions conference is going to be held in Randers this summer to celebrate YWAM's 25th anniversary, and the YWAM Denmark team will now be concentrating all its efforts on helping to organize it. This means I'll now be working in a rotten office while I'm here, instead of travelling round Denmark. Groan. (And 'shiver' as well. It's numbingly cold here at the moment.)

I have three main goals for the next six months: 1) to lose weight; 2) to learn the Danish language;

and 3) to remember the names of all the people I'll be working with.

I think I'll especially need prayer for goal number three.

20th January (Sunday):

I was having a lot of doubts today about whether I've done the right thing by coming here, but Per Eivind cheered me up a bit by describing this conference (called the GO Festival) to me in more detail. About 5,000 Christians from all over the world are expected to attend, and a lot of famous Christian speakers and musicians have been booked already (including Loren Cunningham, the founder and President of Youth With A Mission). It sounds terrific, but it's still six months away. What will I be doing until then?

After being filled up with pancakes this afternoon, I took my doubts for a walk in the cold and bumped into one of Lisbeth's friends whom I met the last time I was here. He invited me back to his flat and *also* filled me up with pancakes. By the time I went to bed I had pancakes (and that Mars bar I'd had on the way into town) on the brain.

I solemnly swore this evening not to have any more Mars bars until after the GO Festival. I put some weight on again in California, and I need to look good when I meet all these Christian celebrities in the summer.

21st January (Monday):

I went for a walk in the freezing cold again this morning, then spent the rest of the day trying to thaw out in my bedroom while reading *Is That Really You, Lord?*, a book by Loren Cunningham on the history of YWAM. I also called Mum in California, and she told me how warm it is there. I tried to pretend I was enjoying myself.

Apart from Liv Ella and myself, three other people are living in this flat: a couple who have just completed a YWAM School of Evanglism in London (the wife is Danish, and the husband is Swiss-German), and Solfrid, Ellinor Stig's sister.

I like having two Norwegians in the flat. They let me eat their Norwegian goat cheese.

22nd January (Tuesday):

I did my first official work for the GO Festival today. It wasn't very much—just helping to paint the office for a few hours—but at least it was something. The office is next to a cattle market, so we get the smell of cows drifting in every day. It's worse than the smell of that rat in Holmsted Manor's tape department!

I also got to meet some other members of staff. There are only eleven people on the permanent YWAM Denmark team who'll be staying here after the festival, so most of the GO Festival staff will be made up of volunteers from different European YWAM bases. There aren't too many here at the moment, but I've been told that there'll be over 300 on the staff by the time the festival starts!

I was desperate for something to eat after all the painting, so I treated myself to a Mars bar. I don't care about that vow I made two days ago. I was absolutely famished.

23rd January (Wednesday):

More painting today, and during break-time I bought myself a Danish *Spider-Man* comic which I'm going to slowly translate into English with my Berlitz Danish/English dictionary. Hopefully, I'll be fully conversant in the Danish language by the time I reach the end.

This evening all of us on the staff met to talk about the plans for the GO Festival so far, and also to officially introduce ourselves to each other. They all seem a great bunch of people, and I'm glad to have now met all of them even though I still can't remember some of their names. At least they now all know who *I* am, which must count for something.

I finally feel like I'm settling in. Praise the Lord!

24th January (Thursday):

Today—as with most days this week—I went from glorious highs of extreme euphoria to terrible lows of deep depression, and I felt very lonely. I miss the camaraderie that comes from going into Christian battle with similarly-aged people, but so far I don't see much of that happening this year. Also, I need a person of my age (and the same sex) with whom I can share problems intimately. Most of the people here are married couples who have problems of their own. I talked my frustrations over with a visitor from the London YWAM base this evening, and she suggested that maybe God is teaching me to depend more on him and less on other people. I think she's right.

I finished another YWAM book this evening, called *To Munich With Love*. It chronicles the YWAM outreach to the Olympic Games in 1972, and it's made me even more thirsty for that sort of work. That goat cheese sandwich I had while reading it also made me thirsty.

25th January (Friday):

Today was a breakthrough day for me. So many good things happened. Someone on the Denmark team bought me some coat hangers and a pair of green mittens, I received a letter from Scotland which brought back many happy memories of *Blake's 7*, and I had an excellent evening meal at Jan's house.

The main thing that caused the breakthrough, however, was the special meeting that the permanent Denmark team had this evening. Basically, it was to explain why we need to concentrate totally on the preparations for the GO Festival. One of the words mentioned (well, two words actually) was 'identity crisis', which is exactly what I've been going through these last few days. Most of the team arrived here expecting to do one thing, and now find they'll be doing something entirely different. This was all clarified in the meeting, and we were also given a lot of much-needed encouragement. Praise the Lord!

26th January (Saturday):

Lots of fun and games in the pantry today.

The top of the hot water tap popped off this morning when I turned it on, and it took me a whole minute to force it back on again. In the meantime, scalding hot water was shooting up out of the pipe at three times the speed of sound, soaking the ceiling and absolutely everything else in the room (including me and all the previously-dry laundry on the indoor washing line).

Two hours later I had to get some water again, but this time I went for the cold tap. Unfortunately I bumped into the hot tap and the top shot off again. What a sight to behold! The top refused to stay on this time, so for the next five minutes the Swiss chap in our flat and I desperately tried to block up the pipe with our hands (firstly), some old rags (secondly), and a broom handle (last). None of these were very effective, so we eventually had to fetch a neighbour to turn off the water supply for us (which we didn't know how to do).

I *was* going to have a bath this evening, but didn't see the point after getting drenched. So instead I set about learning Danish from my *Spider-Man* comic, and translated a phenomenal three-and-a-half words. I'm going to have to get a more comprehensive Danish/English dictionary.

27th January (Sunday):

I missed church this morning because I accidentally woke up too late. (Actually, I woke up at just the right time, but was too lazy to get out of bed.) When I eventually got up I tried to have a quiet time instead, and sort of fell asleep with my Bible over my face. Oh well.

Solfrid, Liv Ella and I have made an agreement. None of us are allowed to eat chocolate until Friday, and the penalty for breaking this is running to town and back in less than forty-five minutes. We're also not allowed to tell anyone else about what we're doing—but I'm telling you, dear diary, because I can trust you.

28th January (Monday):

Today was the official opening day of the GO Festival office in Randers. The Denmark team and the GO Festival lot got together in the morning for a time of praise and worship, and then I spent most of the rest of the day helping to fold and collate the Danish-language GO Festival leaflets.

I absent-mindedly bought a Mars bar this lunchtime, then remembered Sunday's chocolate agreement after I'd eaten it. The next few days I'm going to have to be very secretive and go out of my way to avoid Solfrid and Liv Ella. I know this is wrong, but it's better than running to town and back in less than forty-five minutes.

29th January (Tuesday):

I'm really excited about being a part of this GO Festival. It will be a great week of fellowship and sharing as thousands come together to exalt God and to extend his kingdom on earth, and many lives will be changed as people are challenged to enter into a deeper commitment to him. Tremendous!

I collated leaflets in the office again today. I still don't know what I'll be doing here during the next six months.

30th January (Wednesday):

I spent some time with a few of the GO Festival bigwigs today as they discussed all the jobs that need to be done before and during the festival. My brain was whirling by the time I left them, and I hadn't realized before just what a mammoth operation this is. I need to start praying more for the success of this festival instead of being mostly just an observer.

My brain is deteriorating. I was watching a cookery programme at the Stigs' flat this evening, and it took me a whole five minutes to realize that it wasn't in English. I wonder if chocolate kills brain cells.

31st January (Thursday):

I went to Amigo Burger (the main fast-food place in town) this lunchtime, and had a strawberry milk shake and a spring roll (or *kinarulle*). Then I brought a cream cake and another strawberry milk shake into the office, and started reading chapter seventeen of *The Screwtape Letters* by C. S. Lewis.

With cake inside my mouth and cream all over my nose and fingers, I was horrified to discover that the chapter was all about gluttony.

Conviction of sin is a terrible thing. No more snacks for you, Andrew! You need to discipline yourself!

I have a strong craving for goat cheese right now. I'm sure Liv Ella won't mind if I take two or three slices from the fridge...or four....

1st February (Friday):

Praise God! The chocolate agreement is now over, and no one asked me if I'd eaten any these last few days. So now I can go back to eating Mars bars without feeling guilty. Hooray!

I finished folding and collating the GO Festival leaflets yesterday, so today I had something new to do: stuffing the leaflets into envelopes.

I'm bored. I wish we could do something more exciting.

2nd February (Saturday):

Solfrid asked me today if I'd like to join her, Liv Ella and the Dane in our flat on a week-long trip to a town called Naestved, ministering to a youth group there and telling them about the GO Festival. 'Yes!' I screamed. 'Anything for a break from the office!' And I danced around the flat for the next few minutes, shouting 'Hallelujah!' and punching all the walls in excitement. (I don't experience euphoria very often, so I like to make the most of it when it happens.)

Solfrid very nearly changed her mind about me going after this (and I don't blame her), but luckily she didn't, and we had our first team meeting in her room this evening. We're going to be meeting a lot this week (we leave a week on Monday), and that on top of the two weekly Denmark team meetings and the meeting for the GO Festival staff every Thursday evening. No wonder some people call YWAM 'Youth With a Meeting'!

3rd February (Sunday):

Like last week, I 'accidentally' missed church again in the morning, but I don't feel too bad about it because I had an unusually good quiet time with the Lord. Then I crashed out on my bed until about 3 pm when Solfrid summoned me to another meeting of the Naestved team.

It looks like we'll be having a lot of fun in Naestved—with one glaring exception. The 'ministering' we'll be doing includes performing rotten dramas. I've never been too good at expressing myself with my body (a typical stiff Englishman), and in one of the dramas ('The Heart Sketch') I have to play a clown. I cringe every time I think of it.

I have three boils on my legs at the moment. I wonder if it's anything to do with all the Mars bars I've been eating?

4th February (Monday):

A miracle happened in the office today.

At the moment the YWAM crowd have only one van for transport, and there's a major complication: it has a German licence plate, and Danes are only allowed to drive foreign-licenced vehicles for two weeks after they come into the country. There is now, therefore, a chronic lack of people in the office to drive it.

I let slip today that I had a California driving licence, and one team member's eyes immediately lit up. 'Aha,' he said. '*You* can drive it!' I was at pains to explain that I hadn't driven for almost a year now, and that I could only drive an automatic vehicle. 'Great,' said the team member. 'I can teach you.'

This is the miracle: they actually wanted me to do an errand this afternoon, but then I discovered that I didn't have my driving licence with me. 'Hallelujah!' I thought. 'I must have left it in America.' However, God has only given me a one-day reprieve. I found it in a draw in my bedroom this evening, so I have to start driving tomorrow.

5th February (Tuesday):

That team member spent two hours with me this afternoon, teaching me how to drive the van. When I got home and looked in the mirror I thought I was developing grey hairs from all the worry. But then I realized that it was only paint from the painting I'd been doing.

There was another YWAM Denmark meeting tonight. Previous meetings have been held in English, but tonight was the first time it was totally in Danish. And since I'm the only non-Danish speaker on the team, Solfrid volunteered to translate for me. It was terrible! Instead of being able to nod off in the corner without anybody noticing, I now had to concentrate totally, and prove I was listening by nodding and grunting at various intervals. I was so exhausted after all this that I went to bed immediately, and I'm writing this diary entry tomorrow morning.

I guess it had to happen eventually. The price of Mars bars has gone up by 50 øre! I either need to believe God for more financial support, or seriously reconsider my food budget.

6th February (Wednesday):

Well, another frustrating day in the office. Everyone's certainly keeping me busy with different odd jobs, but I just don't feel as if I'm being used to my full potential. God must have brought me to Denmark for more than just typing people's letters and painting ceilings. I enjoy working with my fellow YWAMers, but I'm the sort of person who likes to give himself totally to one long-term project rather than just bits and pieces here and there. I know the Lord's got something better for me in Denmark, and I'm praying that I'll be assigned a specific position in the office. The Lord had better answer this prayer soon otherwise I'm going to go crazy.

I did some more driving today, and I felt a lot more confident. Now it's the turn of the people travelling with me to stop getting nervous.

7th February (Thursday):

We now have two vans (one came from Holland yesterday, along with two more GO Festival-type people). The second van refused to start this morning, so we all had a great time pushing it in the snow, redistributing the snow among ourselves (e.g. having snowball fights), and eventually using the 'good' van to pull the other one along with rope until it started. We were laughing about this on the way to work, and someone suggested I should keep a diary of all the funny things that happen during the preparations for the GO Festival. Little do they know.

My boss approached me before I left the office today. An info packet will be sent to everyone who registers for the GO Festival, and he wants me to write the first draft of the introductory letter for it. I'm not very good at writing 'official'-type letters, and I've been worrying about it all evening. Lord, I don't like jobs where you have to think. Why didn't you just let me continue painting and typing other people's letters?

8th February (Friday):

At the advice of Per Eivind and Ellinor, I got regis-
tered into the Danish 'system' today. Basically this
means that I can now have free health care and enjoy
most of the benefits of a Danish citizen. I also don't
have to leave the country every three months to renew
my visa. The main benefit, though, is that I'm not
allowed to drive foreign-licenced vehicles any more.
What a shame.

I also wrote that introductory letter. After a whole
two hours of procrastination in the office—scratching
my head while pretending to think, meticulously
cleaning the typewriter keys, then getting a chocolate
milk shake from Amigo Burger to give me the energy
to type—I finally got the thing done and handed it to
my boss, making excuses for all the flaws. He didn't
have time to read it today, so hopefully I won't see him
again until after Naestved. I'm not looking forward to
him telling me how bad it is.

9th February (Saturday):

A number of us YWAMers got together this evening to
take something called the Myers-Briggs personality
test. I was rather sceptical of this at first, but my result
(I'm an 'intuitive introvert') came out surprisingly
accurate: 'Full of enthusiasms and loyalties, but
seldom talk of these until they know you well. Care
about learning, ideas, language, and independent
projects of their own. Tend to undertake too much,
then somehow get it done. Friendly, but often too
absorbed in what they are doing to be sociable. Little
concerned with possessions or physical surroundings.'

I like the bit about me being little concerned with my physical surroundings. Now I have an excuse for my room always being untidy.

10th February (Sunday):

Someone at church today told me I was cute, and I wasn't sure whether to treat this as an insult or a compliment. We 'intuitive introverts' are obviously very sensitive about these sorts of things.

I'm also very sensitive about playing the clown in that rotten 'Heart Sketch'. Oh well. It's a small price to pay for having a week away from the office.

11th February (Monday):

Our first day in Naestved.

We left Randers this morning at 6.30. It was terrible! Someone put a tape of praise songs on in the car, and all were singing merrily away as we drove to the ferry—except for me, half asleep at the back, with my ears directly in front of one of the blaring speakers. I couldn't understand how everyone could be so happy so early in the morning, and I managed to resist the urge to strangle the next person who smiled at me.

We arrived at Naestved at about 2 pm, and we are staying at the house of an extraordinarily nice couple whose names I can't remember. The husband is from America, which is great news for me because most of the time he speaks in English.

The first meeting with the youth group this evening was very informal, and we used the time to get to know each other. One chap came up to me afterwards and told me he recognized me from 'The Chicken Sketch' which our small team performed on the walking street in Copenhagen last year. I felt exhausted most of the day, especially after waking up so early, but this unexpected encounter was a real encouragement to me. Praise God!

12th February (Tuesday):

Today got off to a slow start. The other members of the team (all of them women) decided to go on a morning shopping expedition, and they asked me if I'd like to go with them. 'Okay,' I agreed, stupidly forgetting that when you go shopping with women you spend most of your time in boring clothes shops. Anyway, I enjoyed the music in those shops, although I don't think Solfrid approved of me dancing around all the time.

The rest of the day was splendid. The four of us had intercession in the afternoon, and I felt a closeness to God that I haven't experienced for a long time. Then in the evening we met with the youth group again. We started off with praise and worship (fantastic!), then Solfrid gave a teaching on 'Overcoming Fear'.

I really appreciate working with this youth group. God is uniting us each day with his love, and there's a warmth and friendliness here which is a tremendous blessing to me. I'm spreading the word about my Mars bar addiction, so that hopefully all these warm and friendly people will buy me some.

13th February (Wednesday):

Solfrid came into my room this morning and was horrified with the way I'd 'made' my bed. I tried to put my untidiness down to cultural differences (e.g. 'That's the way we do it in England'), so she played along with me by showing me how they make beds in Denmark. I promised I would do better tomorrow morning.

In the afternoon we were shown round a ceramics factory where one of the youth group works. Then we had spaghetti and ice-cream (separately, of course) at a couple's house...and then there was another evening meeting with the youth group. Great stuff! Solfrid spoke on 'Self-acceptance', and we felt a real breakthrough in openness among the group.

Our team were mentioned in today's issue of *Naestved Ugebladet*, a local newspaper. I haven't a clue what was written about us, but it's nice to have some recognition. I've made a note to pray for myself in the area of pride. We Christian superstars have to watch out for these sorts of things, you know!

14th February (Thursday):

I learnt something very important today: never drink Coca-Cola when you're eating with people who don't speak English. We had a meal at another couple's house this afternoon, and because I couldn't communicate with them I gobbled my food up very quickly and got through a whole bottle of the aforementioned beverage. I spent the following hour politely smiling at the table while trying to hold back all the burps. It was ever so embarrassing.

I gave my testimony during our meeting with the youth group this evening, and we also premiered 'The Heart Sketch'. Both went surprisingly well (in spite of all my worrying), but I found it hard to focus on God during most of the meeting. The others on the team felt an oppression as well, and Solfrid explained later that since we are doing God's work the devil is trying to bring us down. But God is infinitely stronger than Satan, and we are going to be doing a lot of praying over the next few days against this sort of thing happening again.

Solfrid handed me a Mars bar before going to bed tonight, and it really touched my heart. I wasn't expecting it at all, and it was a definite encouragement to me and my stomach.

15th February (Friday):

I had two embarrassing experiences with the washroom today. I was waiting ouside for Liv Ella to finish brushing her teeth, jokingly moaning at how slow she was, when a hand suddenly emerged from inside and threw a glass of cold water at me. It rather dampened my enthusiasm for Liv Ella. (Pause for laughter.) Another time, I slowly walked out of the washroom to see the Danish team member outside, screaming at me. I'm still shaking now, and that's why my handwriting isn't too good.

The four of us went witnessing on the streets in the evening, which was frustrating for me because most of the conversations we had were in Danish (which meant that my partner did most of the talking). But I enjoyed our meeting with the youth group afterwards. It was wonderfully informal, and we spent most of the time teaching them 'The Chicken Sketch' and a drama called 'The Unforgiving Servant'. (Correction: we spent most of the time fooling around and not actually doing the dramas at all!) We will be performing 'The

Unforgiving Servant' at a church service tomorrow evening.

16th February (Saturday):

Today was a long, but fulfilling day.

We started off with witnessing on the streets (with some of the youth group this time), which I enjoyed even though there was still a language problem. Then we had a time of fellowship and prayer (and also eating) with the leaders of the group. Great stuff!

In the evening we had a large meal with the pastor of the youth group's church, and we participated in the Saturday evening service. There were songs and short testimonies from us, and I played the title role in 'The Unforgiving Servant'. Finally, we spent a relaxing few hours with the couple we're staying with, singing praise songs around the piano and devouring Danish pastries.

It's a shame we have to leave tomorrow. I'm enjoying it here, and I'm especially enjoying all the food! Oh, the sacrifices a missionary has to make....

17th February (Sunday):

It was a sad day for me today. We've made many friends in Naestved and had a lot of good times together, but now it was time for us to leave. After the morning service we hugged or shook hands with nearly everyone in the congregation, and then it was 'Goodbye Naestved'.

I feel close to God again after this week (and also closer to my fellow team members), and I want to praise him for all that happened in Naestved.

Tomorrow it's back to the normal routine again, so feel free to skip a few pages.

18th February (Monday):

Much to my surprise, my boss told me today that he liked that letter I wrote for the GO Festival info packet—and he's given me a *new* writing assignment. I'm now in charge of putting together the forty-page programme/brochure that will be given to everyone who attends the GO Festival, which is a big responsibility.

I wrote up a list this evening of all the items that need to go in the programme: an introduction from either Loren Cunningham or Floyd McClung (the head of YWAM in Europe); a time schedule for the whole week (seminar times, meal times, etc.); a comprehensive list of the seminars and speakers; short biographies of all the main speakers; a map of the housing and seminar locations (the GO Festival participants will be sleeping in different schools and church buildings around town); and a detailed timetable for the transport to and from all these different locations. Added to that, I somehow need to obtain photographs of all the main speakers and musicians—and *everything* has to be translated into five different languages!

So far, the entire staff for the programme is me. There is no editor, no graphic artist, and no one to sell advertising space to different businesses in Randers. If my boss had given me this assignment when I first arrived here, I would have panicked and gone absolutely crazy. But God has been working a lot on my confidence these last few weeks, so now I only went absolutely crazy.

Floyd McClung's Introduction to
the GO Festival Programme:

Dear Friend,

Welcome to the GO Festival!

It is with great joy that I, along with all the others who have worked to make this festival possible, welcome you to Randers for this exciting missions and youth festival.

We believe that it is a great privilege and adventure to be called by God into missionary service. It is for that reason that we have chosen this festival as an opportunity to celebrate God's call to Youth With A Mission and his entire church to fulfil the great commission.

What is the mission field? It is people who do not know Jesus Christ. It is people groups that have not been reached with the gospel. Who is the missionary? Anyone, regardless of age or race, called by God to reach other people with the gospel.

What is missions? It is music. It is preaching. It is evangelism. It is translating the Scriptures. It is drama. It is administration. It is short term. It is long term. In short, it is anything that has to do with fulfilling the great commission.

It is my hope and prayer that the GO Festival will be a turning point in your life.

Yours in Christ,
Floyd McClung, Jr.

*   *   *

22nd July (Monday):

It was the first day of the GO Festival today, and about seventy of the staff are now working in the 'nerve centre', a large room at the back of the Randers-hallen (the main meeting place in Randers where the bulk of the GO Festival meetings will be held). Every department in the GO Festival organization has representatives here (transportation, catering, hospi-tality, etc.), and it's quite hectic today with everyone trying to finish last-minute jobs. Some joker has re-dubbed this room the 'nervous centre', which is quite appropriate!

I finished all my work on the GO Festival pro-gramme a few weeks ago, so now I'm in charge of all the photocopying. I was given a lot to do today from different departments (most of which wanted their copies done 'immediately'), and it was quite exhaus-ting running backwards and forwards between our two photocopying machines, one in a small room at the back of the 'nerve centre' and one in the staff snack room. But my exhaustion disappeared at 7.20 pm when I went to the main hall to deliver a message to some-one. The praise and worship for the opening session had already started, and the atmosphere was incred-ible with 5,000 voices praising the Lord! I had a smile on my face as I walked back to that 'nerve centre', and all the hard slog of the last few months now seems worth while.

It's going to be a busy night tonight. I'll tell you about it tomorrow.

23rd July (Tuesday):

My main responsibility during the GO Festival: after each evening meeting, some of the YWAM bigwigs meet together to figure out which announcements need to be made the following morning. I'm handed these announcements at around 10 pm and I'm then responsible for having them translated into five different languages and photocopying 5,000. Last night didn't go quite as quickly as I'd hoped for as some of the translators couldn't type. This meant I had to type whole pages of announcements that I couldn't understand. I wasn't finished until about 2.30 am, and I had to be back at the Randershallen early this morning to make sure all the copies were left by the two entrances before the first meeting.

It's going to be like this all week. I'm not at my best when I don't get much sleep, and I was in a grouchy mood all day. What got me even more annoyed was the fact that the 'nerve centre' has been invaded by hundreds of flies. I don't know why they're all here. Maybe it's because of all the half-eaten junk food we leave around the place.

To keep me going today, I kept getting Coca-Colas (and Mars bars) from the vending machines in the main hall. Praise God for Coca-Cola and chocolate! I'm not going to be able to survive this week without them.

24th July (Wednesday):

It's great being a member of staff. There are big eating tents outside, and instead of waiting in large queues like everyone else, I'm allowed to stand in the shorter staff queue which means I get my food almost immediately. While waiting today, someone I knew from England handed me two king-size Mars bars and a packet of custard that she'd bought for me as a late birthday present (which was a very pleasant surprise!). Keith, Ida, Lisbeth and Jan are on the staff, and there

148

are a lot of friends from the DTS among the GO Festival participants as well. So this GO Festival is quite a reunion for me.

Things were hectic today. As well as all those announcements, I had to make 5,000 photocopies of a letter to the Greek prime minister to be given out at the evening session. The main speaker this evening was Don Stephens, the director of YWAM's Mercy Ships International. Along with two others, he's been sentenced to three-and-a-half years of prison in Greece for proselytizing (handing a Bible to a Greek boy while helping out with relief efforts after an earthquake). The appeal trial takes place next year, so Don wanted everyone to sign their copy of the letter and send it to Greece as a form of protest. When I'd finally photocopied them all (just minutes before Don was due to start speaking), I quickly signed my own copy of the letter then grabbed a Coke from the machine in the main hall. I needed it to give me energy for the rest of the night's photocopying.

Those flies are still pestering us, and there's one particular fly that doesn't seem to like me. Every time I worked in my room at the back of the 'nerve centre' today he crawled all over my face, trying to get in my ears or up my nose and generally driving me crazy. I kept trying to kill him, but he always managed to fly away just before my palm painfully made contact with my head. Hopefully he'll bother someone else tomorrow.

25th July (Thursday):

Not having much sleep is starting to get to me. Despite drinking about seven cups of strong Danish coffee from the staff snack room, I kept drifting off at both photocopying machines last night, dreaming of pillows and soft warm blankets.

That fly is getting to me as well, and I had a bad dream about him. In it I was quietly working in my photocopying room when he suddenly appeared at the doorway. He was seven feet tall, held a shiny brown briefcase and wore a smart bowler hat.

'Hello,' he said to me, lifting the hat politely. 'My name is Frederick the Fly.' He had a warm, friendly expression on his face. For some reason, I wasn't scared of him in the slightest. It was as if having a seven-foot fly dropping in on you was just a normal everyday occurrence.

'Hello, Frederick,' I said. 'What do you want?'

'Look, I'm sorry about this,' Frederick apologized, looking genuinely regretful, 'but I've been sent here by the Insect League of Denmark to torment you.'

'Oh yes?' I said, calmly putting new paper in the photocopying machine. 'How are you going to do that?'

In answer to this, Frederick's expression changed to one of extreme menace and he opened up his briefcase. He took six custard pies from inside and threw them at me, then took two large water pistols and went: 'Kapow! Kapow! Take that you human!' while squirting them.

'Glub,' I went. (I meant to say: 'What on earth are you doing?' but my mouth was full of water.) Then the fly shrunk to normal size and adventurously explored my face while I kept trying to hit him. This went on until my alarm clock woke me up a few minutes later.

'Thank goodness that was just a dream,' I thought, and after I'd got dressed I walked over to the Randershallen to make sure all the announcements had been left by the entrances again.

A friend from Scotland handed me some comics today, including the latest issue of *The Beano*. I tried to read them in the 'nerve centre' but Frederick kept buzzing from one ear to the other and I was never able to swat him in time.

In the evening I fell asleep a few times at the photo-copying machines again, but Frederick would always kindly wake me up so that I could carry on with my duties. How very considerate of him. (That was sarcasm, in case you hadn't guessed.)

26th July (Friday):

Loren Cunningham came into the 'nerve centre' after lunch today, and I immediately froze in my seat. Two of the staff were showing him around and introducing him to people at different desks.

'C-c-crumbs,' I stuttered, looking at his smiling face at the other end of the room and getting steadily more nervous. There was this great man of God, the world-wide leader of Youth With A Mission whom I'd heard so much about, and he would probably soon be introduced to me. What on earth would I say?

Not wanting to make a complete twit of myself (e.g. nervously dropping things when he eventually got to me and getting all my words muddled up), I quickly finished my fifth Coca-Cola of the day and hid in my small room, hoping that Loren wouldn't be shown inside. Unfortunately Frederick was there to greet me, and he pestered me for a whole half-hour. I hope Loren didn't hear me shouting at Frederick all the time. Maybe *that's* the reason he didn't come in to see me.

How stupid I am. Loren's just a normal person like the rest of us, and he'd probably laugh if he knew what I went through today. I wonder how *he* would react to a tormenting fly?

27th July (Saturday):

I snapped this afternoon in the photocopying room. I couldn't take any more of Frederick bugging me (or insecting me), and I was determined to get rid of him once and for all. Storming out of the room, I snatched a tin of fly spray from one of the desks and chased him round the entire 'nerve centre' with it, shouting madly while climbing over people's desks and chairs in hot pursuit.

Eventually I tripped over a rubbish bin. 'Arrgh!' I screamed as I fell to the ground. And then I explained to all the puzzled, and somewhat concerned, faces that were soon staring down at me: 'Sorry about that. Ha ha. Just trying to kill a fly, that's all.' When I'd put all the rubbish back in the bin I walked back to the photocopying room in shame, only to find Frederick there waiting for me.

'Not you again,' I sighed as he ran in circles round my chin. Absent-mindedly, and without expecting anything to happen, I flicked him. Direct contact! I couldn't believe it! Frederick took his last breath, then plummeted lifeless to the ground.

I looked down at the corpse by my feet and felt slightly bad. I've never liked killing insects, and even though Frederick could be a pain he didn't deserve being crushed between my finger and my chin. 'Poor

Frederick,' I thought.

My regret at his demise didn't last for long. 'Here we go again,' I said as I saw three flies land on the photocopying machine in front of me. 'Help!'

Those flies have been pestering me ever since then. I can't take it any more. They'd better not pester me during my marathon session at the photocopying machines tonight. That will be the last time I have to do it, thank goodness!

28th July (Sunday):

What a great day! A long lie-in this morning, not much work to do in the 'nerve centre' (which meant plenty of time to finish reading those comics I was given on Thursday), and I attended the final evening session in the main hall which was incredible. First, a chap called Paul Clark sang a few songs, then there was praise and worship, and then Arthur Blessitt gave a stirring talk on the importance of having a total commitment to God—something I definitely needed to hear.

You know, those flies haven't bothered me all day— which is a real miracle! For the first time since the start of this festival I could actually sit back and enjoy watching other people being attacked by them!

I only have to spend one more morning in this 'nerve centre'. There's going to be a big clear-up session in here tomorrow.

The GO Festival has finished. Everything I've been working for these last six months...

...is over.

The
Sentimental
Conclusion

5th August (Monday):

Something strange happened a few moments ago. I'm on a train heading away from Randers, and as I listened to music on my Walkman I closed my eyes and imagined film credits rolling up in front of me.

The film had been a good one: a year (on and off) with YWAM as seen through the eyes of someone called Andrew. It was slow in places, and sometimes you wanted to strangle the main character for being so wishy-washy in his relationship with the Lord. But there were enough funny bits along the way to keep you interested, and Andrew experienced a definite growth from the beginning of the film to the end.

Then there were those credits, names rolling by of everyone that Andrew had met this past year: fellow students on the DTS, people he worked with in Copenhagen and in Randers, and others. And then the film was over. Darkness. That's it. Nothing more.

I opened my eyes after this and was surprised to see

that I was still alive. I pinched the back of one of my hands. Yes, I was quite definitely still here, still on this train heading away from YWAM and back to my family in California.

What will I be doing next? I honestly don't know. What I *do* know, however, is that the Lord has plans for me; plans to prosper me and not to harm me, plans to give me a hope and a future (Jeremiah 29:11). I don't want to regard my time in YWAM as my one-year service to God, then spiritually sit back for the rest of my life while waiting for Christ to return. My whole life is a service to God. He hasn't finished with me yet, and this last year was just preparation for whatever he has for me in the future, something that will draw me even closer to him. Isn't that exciting!

Hey, and there's another *Star Trek* film coming out soon as well! Fantastic!

You do not delight in sacrifice, or I would bring it; you do not take pleasure in burnt offerings. The sacrifices of God are a broken spirit; a broken and contrite heart, O God, you will not despise (Psalm 51:16–17).

The spiritual adventure is just beginning....

Is That Really You, Lord?

by Loren Cunningham

As a young man, Loren Cunningham was given a startling vision of waves of young people moving out across the continents, spreading the gospel to a needy and rebellious world.

What did the vision mean? Was it telling him about the future? Was it from God?

In the birth of Youth With a Mission we see how hearing the voice of God can lead to great blessing if we are ready to obey Him in complete trust. As we see how God prepared Loren to tap the energies of young people for the gospel, we are encouraged to look for more of God's supernatural guidance in our own lives.

Loren Cunningham is Director of Youth With a Mission. He lives in Hawaii with his wife and two children. Janice Rogers is Loren's sister and a professional writer.

Kingsway Publications